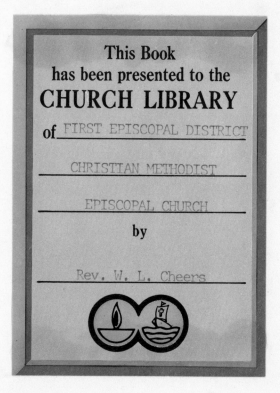

THE STORY OF THE

CHRISTIAN
CHURCH

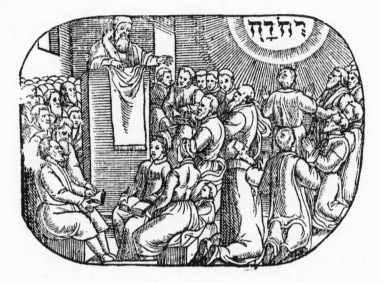

True Christian worship as depicted in John Foxe's *Book of Martyrs*. The preaching of the word and the searching of the Scriptures leads to contrition, trust, and humble supplication in the presence of the God who thus makes himself known to men.

THE STORY OF THE
CHRISTIAN
CHURCH

by Winthrop S. Hudson

HARPER & BROTHERS
Publishers : New York

The illustrations on pages 19, 33, 44, 62, 68, and 70 are reproduced with the permission of the Metropolitan Museum of Art, New York. The publishers are grateful to the staff of the Print Collection at the Museum and to the staffs of the various collections at the New York Public Library for their assistance in selecting the illustrations.

Chapters IX and X are adapted from material which appeared in *Crossroads,* April-June 1957. Copyright 1957, W. L. Jenkins. Used by permission.

Library of Congress Catalog card number: 58-7475

To
study groups
in church and on campus
from
whose ecumenical conversations
I have profited

Contents

Preface   xi

I. The Nature of the Church   1

    1. The Church as the People of God—
        the Church Universal   1
    2. The Church as an Institution—
        particular Churches   3
    3. The Waywardness and Fidelity of the Churches   4

II. The Church of the Martyrs   7

    1. The Early Christian Community   7
    2. The Church Orders Its Life   10
    3. The Church Invokes Apostolic Authority   11
    4. The Seed of the Church   12

III. The Church of the Emperor   16

    1. Triumph or Defeat?   17
    2. The Declining Level of Christian Life   20
    3. A Developing Trust in External Rites
        for Assurance of Salvation   20
    4. Clerical Office as a Bone of Contention   22
    5. The Persecuted Become the Persecutors   24
    6. The Church Loses Its Independence   24

IV. An Imperial Church   27

    1. The Petrine Theory   27
    2. The Struggle for Independence   30
    3. "The Intoxication of Victory"   32

V.   Monks, Friars, and Reformers   38

1. The Recurring Evangelical Witness   38
2. "What Touches All Should Be Approved of All"   42
3. Success and Failure   45
4. A Lesson Still to Be Learned   47

VI.   The Church Recovers Its Life   50

1. The Need of the Church to Recover Its Life   51
2. The Rediscovery of the Church as
   the People of God   55
3. Three Major Convictions   55
4. "Such a Candle as by God's Grace Shall
   Never Be Put Out"   57

VII.   The Reformation Churches   61

1. The Lutheran Churches   63
2. The Church of England   66
3. The Reformed-Presbyterian Churches   68

VIII.   The Post-Reformation Churches   73

1. Congregationalists and Baptists   74
2. Methodists   78
3. The Disciples or "Christians"   80

IX.   The Church Secures Its Freedom   83

1. Enriching a Trading Nation   84
2. Dissent Is Difficult to Suppress
   in an Empty Land   85
3. Theological Foundations of Freedom   87

X.   The Church and the Churches   93

1. The Denominational Theory of the Church   93
2. Paths to Unity   98
3. What of the Future?   99

Chronological Table   102

Index   105

Illustrations

True Christian worship   *frontispiece*

Mob violence in the early Church   13

The conversion of Constantine   18

Jerome in his study translating the Scriptures   19

Ambrose as Bishop of Milan   23

Henry IV at Canossa seeking absolution from
    Hildebrand   33

The signing of the Magna Carta   35

St. Francis of Assisi on his deathbed   39

The Inquisition   44

Avignon and the papal palace   46

The Castle Church at Wittenberg   51

The hawking of indulgences   54

Latimer and Ridley being burned at the stake   59

Martin Luther   62

Thomas Cranner   67

John Calvin   68

John Knox   70

Congregational Meetinghouse   75

George Whitefield   79

John Wesley   80

William Penn   84

Roger Williams' "Bloudy Tenent of Persecution"   86

Federal Hall, New York City   88

Francis Makemie's "Narrative of Imprisonment"   91

Preface

One of the conspicuous features of our time is a renewed interest in the church. This interest finds expression in ecumenical conversations, in student "bull sessions," in informal adult discussions. Everywhere one finds increasing evidence of a strong conviction that the life of the church must be rekindled and that, to this end, there is much to be learned from the experience of the church in the past. The explicit purpose of this little book is to further this interest.

There are, to be sure, many extended and detailed histories of the Christian church, and there are many smaller volumes which tell the vivid and dramatic story of the growth and expansion of the Christian movement. But, valuable as these materials are, they have definite limitations. The standard church history textbooks are much too long and too detailed for casual reading. The narrative accounts, on the other hand, do not raise the significant issues, and consequently provide rather thin fare for the reader who is seeking answers to serious questions.

This book seeks to fill a gap between the two types of available material. It is neither a detailed text nor a dramatic account of the history of the church. It does not pretend to tell the whole story of the church. Its aim is much more modest. It is designed to provoke reflection by raising questions relevant to our time within the context of past Christian experience. What is the church? What lessons may be learned from the past? What is the meaning of these lessons for us? What are we, as members of the Christian community in our day, expected to do? How are we to understand our church and how are we to order its life? It is not enough, however, simply to raise questions. If reflection upon these questions is to be intelligent, basic information is indispensable to understand fully the implications of the issues that have been raised. And this the present volume seeks also to provide.

My students and my colleagues on the faculty at the Colgate Rochester Divinity School have contributed in many ways to the writing of this book. Dean Bernhard W. Anderson of Drew Theological Seminary has provided wise counsel; Professor Sidney E. Mead of the University of Chicago and Professor Robert T. Handy of Union Theological Seminary have both stimulated my thinking as it is reflected in the following pages; and I am especially indebted to the discerning insights of J. H. Nichols in his *Primer for Protestants* (Association Press, 1947) and to Stephen Neill in *The Christian Society* (Harper & Brothers, 1953).

The major portions of Chapters IX and X were first published in *Crossroads* (April-June, 1957) and are reprinted in their present form with the permission of the Board of Christian Education of the Presbyterian Church U.S.A. The letter from the student at Wittenberg in Chapter VI is quoted from Roland Bainton's *Here I Stand* and is reprinted with the permission of the Abingdon Press.

WINTHROP S. HUDSON

Colgate Rochester Divinity School
January, 1958

THE STORY OF THE
CHRISTIAN
CHURCH

I. The Nature of the Church

> Too often we take the "church" for granted, as if everyone knows what we mean when we use the word. Even church history textbooks seldom define what it is whose history they are recounting. This lack of focus introduces a degree of confusion into such discussions, largely rules out incisive analysis, permits few judgments to be made, and makes it difficult for the past to speak to us in terms of wisdom, insight, and guidance.

IF WE ARE to talk about the Church, we must be clear as to what we are talking about. *What do we mean when we use the word "church"?*

Actually, the word "church" may mean many different things. It may mean a building, as when we say: "I am going to church for a meeting." It may mean a service of worship, as when our children write home from camp saying: "We had church this morning." It may mean a local organized congregation of people, as when we say: "I belong to the Central Presbyterian Church." It may mean a denomination, as when we speak of the Methodist Church and the United Lutheran Church and the Protestant Episcopal Church. Or finally, it may mean the totality of all Christians in all ages and in all lands, as when the Edinburgh Conference of 1937 declared: "We agree that the Church is the Body of Christ and the blessed company of all faithful people, whether in heaven or on earth, the communion of the saints."

1. *The Church as the People of God—the Church Universal*

In *The Shepherd of Hermas,* the writer, a second-century Christian, tells of a vision in which he saw a very aged woman arrayed in glittering garments, sitting on a great white chair,

1

The Church is an end; the churches are means. The Church is a pure fellowship, a community of persons, the communion of the saints; the churches are institutions, organizations, ecclesiastical structures. The Church has no beginning; the churches were brought into existence because the blessings of Christian fellowship were not to be once received and then passively enjoyed. The Church is a spiritual home, a fatherland, a colony of heaven upon the earth; the churches are missionary societies seeking to transmit by word and deed God's reconciling love to all mankind.

And yet, while the Church and the churches may be distinguished, they are also related; and the churches have no true life apart from the life they find in the Church. We should be clear at this point. It is only as an organized ecclesiastical institution serves to nurture and sustain the new life in Christ which knits men together in love that it has any real claim to be called a Christian church. It is only as such an organization strives to make real within its corporate life a ministry of forgiveness and reconciliation that it can be said to belong to the Body of Christ.

The problem implicit in the relationship of the Church to the churches may be stated in this fashion. The Church is not an institution, but in the life of the world it cannot escape the necessity of expressing itself in institutional terms. The Church does not live according to the flesh, but it does live in the flesh. Organization is not the essence of the Church, but organization there must be. As the Word of God has no life apart from the outward physical means by which it is communicated, so the Church—an inward community of faith and love—must have its outward form, a form determined by the nature of the inward community which it is designed to express.

3. *The Waywardness and Fidelity of the Churches*

The disconcerting fact of human experience is that a particular church, seeking to make manifest in the life of the world the true community to be found in Christ, has never been what it ideally should be. "We have this treasure in earthen vessels," said the apostle Paul. The church, as an organized society of men, has always been tainted with imperfection.

This has been true from the very beginning. The great word of Martin Luther—"the countenance of the church is the countenance of a sinner"—is true even of the New Testament church. At Corinth a party spirit led to bickering and quarrels. The conduct of the Colossian Christians was the subject of sundry admonitions, and the unfaithfulness of the Galatian community was the occasion of the apostle Paul's letter to them. Even at Jerusalem, precautions had to be taken to make sure that the common fund was justly distributed.

The waywardness of the early Christian communities was their weakness, not their strength. It was the measure of their bondage and not of the freedom they had found in Christ. Their waywardness in no way distinguished them from the world about them. What did distinguish them and set them apart from their contemporaries was the remarkable fidelity which, on the whole, in the midst of their waywardness they displayed to the One who had laid his claim upon them. Their fidelity and not their waywardness was the bridge to heaven by which men and women in the ancient world were brought into touch with God's reconciling love.

QUESTIONS TO THINK ABOUT:

1. What does it mean to say that the Church is not a human institution but the creation of God?

2. Is it possible for anyone but God to discern the boundary of the Church? Can we determine with finality who is and who is not to be numbered among the people of God?

3. How would you determine when to spell "church" with a capital "C" and when with a small "c"?

4. If the intention of God has been to create a people, a community, can there be a solitary Christian? Can a person who seeks to divorce himself from his fellow Christians and stand alone in splendid isolation be regarded as fully Christian?

5. How is the church as an institution or organized fellowship to be distinguished from other fellowships of men?

6. Thinking of the churches as you know them in this country, how would you describe their relationship to the Church? Is the real unity of the Church to be found in organization? If not, where is the unity of the Church to be found?

7. It has been said that the two great duties of a church are faithfulness and repentance. What are some of the evidences of unfaithfulness that should evoke a church's repentance?

SUGGESTIONS FOR FURTHER READING:

There are many books which deal with the nature of the church. One of the most provocative and interesting discussions of this theme is Emil Brunner, *The Misunderstanding of the Church* (Westminster Press, 1953). An equally valuable but briefer exposition of much the same point of view will be found in Chapters 1 and 13 of Stephen Neill, *The Christian Society* (Harper & Brothers, 1953). Other useful studies are Lesslie Newbigin, *The Household of God* (Friendship Press, 1954), and J. Robert Nelson, *The Realm of Redemption* (Epworth Press, 1951). Of the New Testament writings, Ephesians and I Peter will be found especially illuminating.

ii. The Church of the Martyrs

Any attempt to reconstruct the developing life and organization of the early church must begin with an acknowledgment that much of our information is meager and fragmentary, and that there is much that is obscure and uncertain. We have no minute books, no diaries, no journals. But we do have scattered letters, reports, treatises, sermons, church manuals. While we could wish for much additional information, the main lines of development are sufficiently clear.

THE MISSION OF Christ was to summon a remnant of Israel to be the saving instrument of God for the redemption of mankind. To accomplish this purpose, he had gathered about him twelve disciples, corresponding to the twelve tribes of Israel. They were to be his "witnesses." After Christ had been crucified and buried, he appeared again to his disciples—first to Peter and then to the Twelve—confirming his mission and entrusting it to them. They returned to Jerusalem, and there the miracle of Pentecost (Acts 2:1-4) occurred, transforming the small band of disciples into a dynamic community with a message and a life that "turned the world upside down."

1. *The Early Christian Community*

The Christian community sprang from the apostolic witness. Christ was the foundation stone of the community, and the apostles were the "pillars." Without the apostles there could have been no Church, for a historical revelation must be reported and announced by those who were "eyewitnesses" to it. But beyond the stabilizing element of the apostolic testimony, it was a formless community which was gathered by the telling of the Christian story.

What distinguished this early Christian community was not a pattern of organization but a way of life. "Since our persuasion by the Lord," Justin Martyr was later to write, "we who valued above all things the acquisition of wealth and possessions now bring what we have into a common stock and communicate to everyone in need; we who hated and destroyed one another, and on account of their different manners would not share the same hearth with men of another tribe, now, since the coming of Christ, live on intimate terms with them, and pray for our enemies and endeavor to persuade those who hate us to live according to the good precepts of Christ, so that they may become partakers with us of the same joyful hope." This was true from the very beginning. It was a new society that had come into existence in the midst of the old society—a society in which there were no distinctions of race or class or nationality or culture, a society in which no person should ever be in need or want, a society in which the stranger should feel himself welcome and at home, a society open to all men, whether Jew or Gentile, through faith in Christ.

In a sense, it is curious that Christ should have laid down no detailed instructions for the outward organization of the Church. In this respect, life under the New Covenant differed greatly from the minute prescriptions by which the life of Israel was ordered under the Old Covenant. But, in a deeper sense, it is not strange that Christ should have left the outer structure of the Church to be shaped by the growing and changing needs

---

JUSTIN MARTYR: The most eminent of the second-century Greek "apologists," so called because of their efforts to present a reasoned defense of the Christian faith. Justin sealed his testimony with a martyr's death about the year 166.

DIDACHE, or TEACHING OF THE TWELVE APOSTLES: An early church manual or directory. It is reprinted in the first volume of the Library of Christian Classics, C. C. Richardson, ed., *Early Christian Fathers* (Westminster Press, 1953).

CANON OF THE NEW TESTAMENT: The list of those books which have been accepted as most clearly being derived from the

of the Christian community, for to do otherwise would have been to run the risk of diverting attention from his basic concern to foster a true fellowship of persons and of centering it instead upon details of order and organization. Christ had insisted again and again that in the new society there was to be no pre-eminence. When a dispute broke out among the Twelve, after the request of the sons of Zebedee that they be given positions of honor and privilege in the coming kingdom, Jesus acknowledged that in the larger society in which they lived the great ones exercised lordship and authority, but, he reminded them, "it is not so among you." The principle by which they were to be governed was the one which he had so often repeated, that whosover would be chief among you shall be a servant.

Thus the outward structure of the Church grew out of the needs of daily life—the sociological needs of individual Christian communities. Actually no fellowship can exist without accepted patterns of doing things and getting things done. Means of conducting business must be devised. In the early church, we can see this process clearly at work in the appointment of "deacons" at Jerusalem to look after the common fund (Acts 6:1-6). The occasion of their appointment was the complaint of the Greek-speaking Christians that their widows were being neglected in the daily distribution of food. To make sure that there would be no just cause for complaint, seven of the Greek-

---

apostles, and which can thus be regarded as containing the authentic teaching of the apostles. Curiously enough, the canon was never defined or determined by a General Council, and only a few local synods ever considered the question as to what books might properly be regarded as canonical.

PERSECUTIONS: For two centuries the persecution of Christians was largely local and sporadic. The great general persecutions which sought to stamp out the Christian communities in systematic fashion occurred under Decius and Gallus in 250-253, Valerian in 257-260, and Diocletian and Galerius in 303-311.

speaking Christians were assigned to look after this particular task.

2.   *The Church Orders Its Life*

It has been suggested that "the early churches lived like those on the American frontier." There was no trained clergy. Scattered groups of Christians had been gathered by itinerant evangelists. These itinerants were the ministers, and their duties involved preaching or prophesying and the administration of baptism and the Lord's Supper. They had been commissioned directly by the Spirit, and they were attached to no local congregation.

All the believers who had been gathered by the itinerants were styled "brethren" or "saints," and each member of the community was regarded as a "priest" belonging to the spiritual tribe of Levi. As in all communities, however, there were certain routine tasks to be performed. Someone had to determine when and where they should meet, to make the necessary preparations, and to preside once the people were gathered together. Also the financial affairs of the community had to be supervised. Following Jewish custom, these administrative responsibilities were usually assumed by a committee of elders—called "bishops" or "presbyters"—and in some places they were assisted by "deacons" and "widows." The pattern of administration, however, was far from standardized. In some centers the committee structure persisted well into the second century. In other centers this pattern of organization was displaced by what seemed to be the more efficient procedure of concentrating responsibility in a single pastor or overseer, and the committee of elders was reduced to the status of an advisory council.

The itinerants often presented something of a problem to the established communities. In time some of them became suspected of abusing their ministerial office. The apostle Paul suggested that true prophets and teachers could be distinguished in part by the evidence they gave of possessing "the fruits of the Spirit." The *Didache* was even more explicit when it suggested that, if the preaching or prophesying of an itinerant ended in a demand for food and money by way of reward, he was to be cast out as a deceiver. The problem posed by the itinerants was ultimately solved by having the bishop or pastor gradually extend his responsibilities to include those of the ministerial office, thus largely displacing the itinerants in the life of the church.

At the same time that the bishop was assuming the duties of the minister, his responsibilities were also undergoing geographical extension. In various important centers the Christian community had enjoyed marked growth and had become too large to meet in one place. Thus it became necessary for the community to divide itself into several distinct congregations meeting in different parts of the city. The bishop or the pastor remained as head of the whole enterprise but presbyters were assigned to take charge of the individual assemblies. And when missionary activity was extended into the neighboring rural areas creating Christian groups there, these too were brought under his supervision.

3. *The Church Invokes Apostolic Authority*

The Christian communities were increasingly troubled by controversy as the years went by. Strange and novel prophetic revelations led to differing interpretations of the person and work of Christ and of the nature of the life to which the Christians had been called. Thus the gospel seemed in danger of being corrupted and perverted, and the whole movement was threatened with disintegration. To meet this danger, an appeal was made to the apostolic witness as the source of the normative tradition of the church.

After the death of the apostles, many writings had appeared, designed to provide the church with authoritative instruction. As was to be expected, the theological speculation and creative imagination which had led to controversy was reflected in this literature. Thus the conflict between the new teachings of those who claimed direct revelations by the Spirit and the long-familiar traditions of the church was heightened. To provide a dependable check against novel doctrines, the principle was seized upon of limiting authoritative teaching to those writings which most clearly could be regarded as being derived from the apostles. As "eyewitnesses" to the life, death, and resurrection of Christ, the apostles provided the only reliable historical evidence concerning the divine disclosure. Their teaching, therefore, was the only trustworthy authority for the church. It was the touchstone by which the true could be detected from the false. All else which claimed the authority of the Spirit must be tested by the teaching of the apostles. While there continued to be differences of opinion among the scattered Christian communities with regard to a few of the books which were ultimately included in the New Testament canon, there was a remarkable degree of unanimity with regard to most of the writings which were judged to be apostolic and thus the source of the normative tradition. When one compares the writings which were rejected with those which were accepted, it is impossible not to be impressed by the sound historical discrimination and judgment that was displayed in the selection made.

4. *The Seed of the Church*

During the years when the Christian communities were ordering the outward form of their common life and seeking stability by an appeal to apostolic authority, they were living a precarious existence. Persecution had begun with the stoning of Stephen (Acts 7:58-60), and for three hundred years the threat of mob violence or more drastic action by the state was to hang over their heads.

It seems curious to us that the early Christians should have been persecuted—whipped, stoned, cast to the lions, condemned to the stake—for by our standards they seem to have been inoffensive enough. The sum of their offense was that they were different. They were living in the world and for the world, but they were not of the world. Their ultimate loyalty was elsewhere.

Because the Christians were different, vicious rumors circulated concerning them. What dark deeds were thought to take place behind the closed doors of their "love feasts." Because Christians were different, it was easy to make them the scape-

Christian preaching often provoked mob violence

goats for every disaster that occurred. Whenever there was flood or drought, famine or pestilence, the cry would be raised: "The Christians to the lions." Because the Christians were different, homes were disrupted and family ties were broken. The greatest offense of the Christians, however, was that they would not worship the gods upon whose favor the welfare of the state was thought to depend. Nor would they acknowledge Caesar as Lord. They made clear again and again that their loyalty was always and only to Christ. It was a loyalty which overrode all other claims of the community upon them.

Stubborn and obstinate in their refusal to perform the rites on which the safety, security, and prosperity of the state were thought to depend, the Christians could only be regarded as traitors to society, worthy of the martyrdom to which they were condemned. Some were slaves, some were inconspicuous folk, some were distinguished leaders of the church. How many there were, no one knows. But there were many who withstood the temptation to deny their Lord.

Was martyrdom necessary? No one can answer that question except for himself when it is his own life that is at stake. It is only in the agony of one's own soul that a Christian determines what the decision for Christ and his kingdom must be. But a Christian must be different, and the Christian society, which is the Church, must be different. And because this is so, the Church must expect the recurrent hostility of those with whom it cannot finally make a compromise. This much is clear: the Christian Church during its days of martyrdom could be neither defeated nor suppressed. The gates of hell could not prevail against it. The very blood of the martyrs became the seed of the Church.

QUESTIONS TO THINK ABOUT:

1. If it is true that Christ left no detailed instructions for the outward organization of the Church, does this mean that questions of church organization are to be regarded as of little consequence?

2. What were the characteristics of church life on the American frontier? What parallels to the early church do you find in the frontier situation?

3. If precedents can be found in the early church for the Baptist and Congregationalist, the Presbyterian and the Episcopal types of church organization, on what grounds must debates as to the proper form of church organization be settled?

4. It is frequently said that the church wrote the Bible, i.e., that the Christian community shaped the writings and determined the canon. Does this mean that the church is free to rewrite the Bible or to alter the canon?

5. Was the early church justified in being disturbed by doctrinal novelties? Many of the proponents of the novel views led exemplary lives. Is not the way one lives more important than correctness of belief?

6. If the mission of the church is to redeem society and culture as well as the individual, can the isolation of the Christian community from the larger community in which it exists be defended? At what point must the Christian limit his participation in the general life of the community and be prepared to pay the consequences?

SUGGESTIONS FOR FURTHER READING:

The best brief statement of the developing organization of the early church is the chapter by John Knox. "The Ministry in the Primitive Church," in H. Richard Niebuhr, ed., *The Ministry in Historical Perspectives* (Harper & Brothers, 1956). A detailed account will be found in Hans Lietzmann, *A History of the Early Church,* Vol. II, *The Founding of the Church Universal* (Charles Scribner's Sons, 1938). Possible source readings include the *Didache,* an early church manual, and the *Martyrdom of Polycarp.* These documents are reprinted in Vol. I of the *Library of Christian Classics* (Westminster Press, 1953), in Henry Bettenson, *Documents of the Christian Church* (Oxford University Press, 1947), and in B. J. Kidd, *Documents Illustrative of the History of the Church* (The Macmillan Company, 1938). The important report of Pliny to Trajan is reprinted in the latter two collections.

III. The Church of the Emperor

One of the "most profound revolutions" which has occurred "in the entire history of the church," W. E. Garrison has declared, was the transformation of the church, in the fourth century, from "a voluntary society having in its membership only those who were members by their own choice" to "a society conceived as necessarily coextensive with the civil community and endowed with power to enforce the adherence of all members of the civil community." The following discussion attempts to make clear the consequences of this revolution in the life of the church.

FOR THREE HUNDRED YEARS Christians had lived in danger of mob violence, and toward the end of this period mob action and local persecution had been replaced by a concerted effort to destroy the Christian movement as a whole. Then, with dramatic suddenness, the precarious position of the Christian communities within the Roman Empire was brought to an end. Almost overnight Christianity emerged from its status as an illegal faith into the role of being the favored and then the official religion of the Empire.

The Emperor Constantine had acted on the basis of the old political maxim—"if you can't beat them, join them." The policy of persecution had failed. Far from being suppressed, the Christian communities had spread and multiplied. Other emperors had sought to make the Empire strong by destroying the Christian communities. Constantine, finding himself in a difficult situation, tried the opposite policy. He decided that his position might be strengthened by enlisting the Christian God in his service. The gamble paid off, his opponents were defeated, and in anticipation of further benefits to be derived from the Christian God, Constantine took the church under

16

his protection, showered it with favors, and assumed responsibility for directing its affairs.

1. *Triumph or Defeat?*

Constantine's conversion to Christianity has frequently been interpreted as a triumph for the church. It is true that Christianity's new status in society did represent at least one definite gain. Persecution is not a blessing, and the individual Christian could now profess his faith openly and without fear. He could meet freely with his fellow Christians for purpose of worship. Imperial favor and patronage represent more dubious gains. The churches were relieved of certain taxes, ecclesiastical courts were recognized, the clergy were exempted from municipal obligations, and grain was given them to distribute to the poor. Public funds were appropriated to build new houses of worship, and the treasures of pagan temples were transferred to them. The lament of Jerome that "the holy books of the Christians which once were given to the flames are now bound in purple and inlaid with gold and jewels" is one indication of the dramatic shift in fortune which had taken place. From obscurity and peril, the church had traveled the road to security, privilege, and favor.

There were other consequences flowing from imperial patronage which suggest that the new position which Christianity had acquired was something less than a full triumph. "The extraordinary change by which Christianity, instead of being the religion of a persecuted minority, became the religion of the Imperial Court," says Edwyn Bevan, ". . . made a greater difference to the character of Christianity than it did to the character of the world. . . . The disappointing thing is that when the change came about, the world went on very much as before —the institutions of the state were the same, the behavior of men in business and pleasure, slavery, wars." But the church did not go on as before. The church was not the same. "The church," as Kenneth E. Kirk, former bishop of Oxford, observed, was "all but completely assimilated to the model of the world."

It was later reported that before the decisive battle Constantine beheld a vision of the Cross with the words: "In this sign conquer."

Jerome in his study translating the Scriptures.
A sixteenth-century engraving by Albrecht Dürer.

2. *The Declining Level of Christian Life*

One of the consequences of fateful future significance which flowed from Constantine's conversion to Christianity was the vast increase in the number of Christians. "It was inevitable," comments John Baillie, "that the majority of Romans would themselves desire to follow the emperor in embracing the new faith. . . . And where Rome led the rest of the Empire would be likely to follow." The ambitious could easily see the political and social advantage to be gained by accepting the emperor's religion, and those who entertained no particular ambitions had long been accustomed to expressing their loyalty to the emperor by worshiping the emperor's gods. Few among the new adherents were more than nominal Christians and many were as pagan as ever at heart. Thus the "high visibility" which had characterized the early Christian communities was obscured and it became increasingly difficult to tell the Christian from the non-Christian.

3. *A Developing Trust in External Rites for Assurance of Salvation*

The general decline in the level of life within the post-Constantinian church accentuated the tendency to seek an external

---

CONSTANTINE: Assumed administration of the provinces of Gaul, Spain, and Britain in 306; marched into Italy and defeated Maxentius in 312, becoming sole ruler in the West. By defeating Licinius in 323, Constantine became ruler of the whole Empire. He summoned the Council of Nicea in 325 and established the new capital of Constantinople in 330.

JEROME: A distinguished scholar, noted as translator of the standard Latin (*Vulgate*) version of the Bible. He was baptized at Rome in 360, became a monk in 373, and spent the last thirty-four years of his life, prior to his death in 420, as head of a monastery in Bethlehem.

AMBROSE: Elected bishop of Milan by popular acclamation in

assurance of salvation. The church could no longer pretend to be a fellowship of the redeemed—a new society of men markedly different in character from the larger society about it. The minimum standard of behavior which could be required of so heterogeneous a company as now constituted the church was not sufficiently rigorous to cultivate the illusion of spiritual security. In this situation, the only way by which the necessity for personal repentance and humble submission in trust to God could be evaded was to place one's reliance upon the efficacy of the rites of the church to secure the blessings of heaven.

One curious phenomenon was the postponement of baptism until the final moments of one's life—a custom which became a common practice. There were many who were not anxious to incur the apparent risk involved in postbaptismal sin. Following the example of Constantine, they delayed their baptism until the moment death was at hand, when there would be little opportunity for them to fall from grace. This was not an entirely satisfactory solution to their problem, for they might either wait too long to be baptized and be thwarted by a sudden death or unexpectedly recover from what they had thought to be a mortal illness and be exposed to the continuing temptations of earthly existence. Ultimately an adjustment was made by introducing the sacrament of penance to take care of postbap-

---

374, when, as governor of the region, he entered the church to preserve order at the election. He was baptized the next day, inducted successively into the various minor orders, ordained a priest, and consecrated bishop a week later. Although famous as a preacher and hymnologist, his great talent was ecclesiastical administration. He immediately became the dominant figure in the church in Italy, did not hesitate to assert its independent status, and was frequently in conflict with the civil authorities. His greatest triumph was his successful disciplining of the Emperor Theodosius.

THEODOSIUS: Emerged as one of the dominant rulers in the Empire in 379, and finally succeeded in reuniting the Empire for the last time in 394. After his death a year later, the imperial authority in the West rapidly disintegrated.

tismal sins and by the use of extreme unction to prepare the soul for death.

The mood which was reflected in the increasing dependence upon the rites of the institution is not unlike that of some modern Protestants who achieve what they believe to be real spiritual security by attending Sunday morning worship regularly and making a generous pledge to the support of the church. It is a relationship to an institution which constitutes for them the badge of a Christian. The men and women of an earlier day were merely somewhat more imaginative in defining practices by which their piety could be demonstrated and merit accumulated.

4. *Clerical Office as a Bone of Contention*

A direct consequence of the reliance upon the rites and ceremonies of the church was the creation of a sharp cleavage between the clergy and the laity. During the fourth and fifth centuries, the laity increasingly became onlookers rather than participants in the actual life of the church. The number of communicants dwindled, and by the sixth century the custom of habitual communion had almost disappeared. The service was performed for them rather than by them. The concept of the church as a community of the faithful was fading and being replaced by the concept of the church as a clerical institution.

The gap between the clergy and the laity was further accentuated by the privileges which Constantine and his successors bestowed upon the clergy. In the early days, the men who presided in the communal acts of worship were in ordinary life indistinguishable from other members of the Christian community. For the most part, they supported themselves by some secular employment. All this was changed when the churches became wealthy and privileged institutions. Regular salaries were assigned to the clergy from funds derived from the confiscated properties of pagan temples and from appropriations by the state. Immunities of various sorts from burdens borne by ordinary men, which previously the pagan priests had enjoyed, were conferred upon the Christian clergy. In addition, the clergy were given certain disciplinary powers over the lives of the people, and the sanctuary rights of pagan temples were extended to include the Christian churches. Thus the clergy constituted a privileged, influential, and frequently wealthy class in society, and a clerical career was to be coveted for reasons quite divorced from any real religious concern. Disgraceful scenes of conflict and disorder not infrequently accompanied an election to the more important posts within the church. Scarcely more than fifty years after Constantine had issued the Edict of Milan, Ambrose as governor

Ambrose as Bishop of Milan

of Milan thought it necessary to be present with his troops at the election of the local bishop in order to preserve order and avoid bloodshed. This was no unnecessary precaution, for only a few years earlier the election of Damascus as bishop of the church in Rome had provoked a pitched battle between the adherents of the contending parties, and before it was over a hundred corpses littered the floor of the church. After Damascus had made good his election by such slaughter, the pagan prefect of the city is reported to have said to him: "Make me bishop of Rome, and I will turn Christian at once."

5. *The Persecuted Become the Persecutors*

Thus far the Christian church had simply been recognized as a legal religion and had been the recipient of official patronage and favor. It was but a short step, however, from official approval and patronage of one religion to discrimination against other religions. Before the end of the fourth century, the Emperor Theodosius had issued an edict which began with the words: "It is our desire and *will* that all the peoples which are governed by the moderation of our clemency should follow the religion which was given to the Romans by St. Peter the Apostle." Christianity was now compulsory, conversion was henceforth to be largely by the sword, and the persecuted were to be the persecutors.

With the exception of concessions which were ultimately to be made to the Jews and the Moslems, every member of society was henceforth to be required to make a Christian profession. The non-Christian and even the unorthodox Christian were to be outlaws, having no rights, living outside the protection of the laws, and subject to immediate execution if apprehended. The ultimate identification of the Christian society with the political community has been described by Sir Ernest Barker in these words: "The excommunicated person could not enter either the church or the law court; could not receive either the eucharist or a legacy; could not own either a cure of souls or an acre of soil." As J. N. Figgis describes the fully developed system, there were no non-churchmen, "or if there were, they were occupied in being burnt." Christianity had become a faith to be maintained and perpetuated by coercion, by the exercise of police power and the utilization of the sword.

6. *The Church Loses Its Independence*

Perhaps the most serious consequence of Constantine's action in assuming the role of protector and patron of the Christian church was the loss by the church of its freedom. "As an emperor who without benefit of clergy or sacraments had chosen to serve the Supreme Divinity whom the church professed to worship"—to use the vivid words of Shirley Jackson Case—

Constantine "felt no hesitation in chiding schismatics, giving orders to clerics . . . , or addressing the most august Christian assemblies convened by his authority." Even though he had not been baptized, Constantine assumed the right to call synods of the church and to enforce their decisions, to intervene in the appointment of the clergy and to serve as final judge of their actions. Nor did he hesitate to dismiss and banish those who ran counter to the policy which he adopted for the church. Henceforth the church was to be regarded as an arm of the government. This state of affairs was to continue in the eastern portion of the Empire until its collapse on the eve of the Reformation, and it has been perpetuated to the present day in some of the Eastern churches, and to varying degrees in the Church of England and the various Lutheran territorial churches. The most conspicuous modern illustrations of the unhappy consequence of this tradition are to be found in the events which befell the church in Russia during the Revolution and in Germany under the Nazi regime, but the control of the Church of England by Parliament, however benevolent that control has been, has not been an altogether happy situation.

QUESTIONS TO THINK ABOUT:

1. Are churches always in danger when they become respectable, popular, and prosperous?

2. What would you consider to be the most unhappy consequence of dependence by the churches upon state support?

3. Are there social pressures today which may result in increased church membership without any corresponding depth of Christian conviction? Are there business, political, and social advantages to be gained by joining a church?

4. What is the relationship of participation in the rites of the church to the Christian life?

5. Why is the freedom and independence of the church important?

6. In your experience, is there a clear-cut tension between the church and the world? What is wrong with the contention that religion belongs in one sphere and political and economic issues in another?

SUGGESTIONS FOR FURTHER READING:

A brief account of the life of Constantine is to be found in S. J. Case, *Makers of Christianity* (Henry Holt and Co., 1934), and the effect of the Constantinian revolution upon the life of the church is described by Stephen Neill in the third chapter of *The Christian Society* (Harper & Brothers, 1953). An extended treatment of the period is provided by Hans Lietzmann, *History of the Early Church*, Vol. III, *From Constantine to Julian* (Charles Scribner's Sons, 1950). Relevant documentary materials will be found in Henry Bettenson, *Documents of the Christian Church* (Oxford University Press, 1947), pp. 22-28, 31-32.

IV. An Imperial Church

The Christian church has had a strange odyssey, and one of the most remarkable chapters in its history was the attempt to fashion an imperial church to rule the world. The aim was to introduce order, peace, and unity into a society that was badly disordered and plagued by constant strife. In the pursuit of this goal, the church itself became infected by the evil which it sought to cast out.

KENNETH SCOTT LATOURETTE has characterized the period from 500 to 1500 as "the thousand years of uncertainty." It was a period of confusion, when expressions of Christian faith and life were multiform and variegated, when strife and conflict were endemic, when changes occurred so slowly as to be almost imperceptible. One conspicuous feature of these ten centuries, however, was an attempt to fashion an imperial church to replace the Empire, which had crumpled in the West. As a result of its close connection with the Empire, the church had developed an organization along the lines of the Empire—with dioceses, provinces, and an incipient tendency in some quarters of the West to centralize authority in the hands of a single ruler, the bishop of Rome.

1. *The Petrine Theory*

The pre-eminence of Rome among the churches of the West is easily to be understood. Rome was the imperial capital, the Eternal City, the only major city in the West; and the Roman church was the largest and wealthiest church, with a reputation for orthodoxy and charity. In addition, while several churches in the East could claim an apostolic foundation, this was true of Rome alone in the West. As the back-country churches of colonial Massachusetts and even the Presbyterian churches of colonial New Jersey frequently appealed to the ministers of Boston for counsel and advice in their controversies, so the churches of an earlier day often looked to Rome for help in settling their differences. But even men, like Irenaeus and Cyprian, who supported the leadership of Rome in the defense of orthodoxy did not hesitate to dissent when they felt that Rome was in error. The bishops of Rome, on the other hand, tended to feel that they had peculiar prerogatives which ought not to be slighted.

To support the Roman pretensions Leo I, in the middle of the fifth century, developed a theory of Petrine succession based upon the text: "Thou art Peter and upon this rock I will build my church" (Matt. 16:18). The theory was that Peter was the prince of the apostles to whom had been given authority over the other apostles and the church, that Peter was the first bishop of Rome, and that his authority had been transmitted to succeeding bishops of Rome. This was not a succession of persons, as was true of the theory of apostolic succession, but

LEO I: Bishop of Rome (440-461), whose great service was assuming leadership for the total community of Rome during the invasions of the Huns and Vandals.

GREGORY I (the Great):   Bishop of Rome (590-604), a monastic of deep piety, who raised troops for the defense of Rome when his appeals to the distant emperor for help against the Lombards were unavailing.

CHARLEMAGNE: Became king of the Franks in 768; vastly extended his domains; became the protector of the bishop of Rome, defeating the Lombards, and was crowned emperor by the bishop of Rome in 800. The two parties interpreted the meaning of this act differently. Charlemagne interpreted it as giving him the status of Constantine, called of God to rule in state and church. Succeeding bishops of Rome understood it to mean that they could make and, if need be, unmake emperors. Thus from it stems both the idea of the divine right of kings and the concept of the temporal power of the papacy.

a succession in office. The authority was not conveyed from one occupant of the office to another by the laying on of hands, for an interval always occurred between the death of a bishop of Rome and the election of his successor.

There were several difficulties in making use of this text for such a purpose. First, Peter had just confessed his conviction that Jesus was the Messiah, and the majority of church fathers were in agreement that the "rock" upon which the Church was established was not Peter but the conviction he had expressed. Second, the Gospels make it clear that pre-eminence among the followers of Christ was not to be after the pattern of the princes of the world who exercise lordship and authority, but in terms of humble service. Third, Peter continued to be notoriously unstable, being immediately rebuked by Jesus and called Satan for not understanding "the things that be of God," denying his Lord in the moment of crisis, being supplanted by James as leader of the Jerusalem community, and being criticized by Paul as an unreliable disciple. Fourth, the theory assumes that the grant of authority was not to Peter but to

---

HILDEBRAND (Gregory VII): Bishop of Rome (1073-1085), one of the mighty men of history whom, it is said, even Napoleon envied. For fifteen years prior to his own elevation he was the real power in the Roman church, charting its course and directing its activities. He is most commonly remembered for the incident at Canossa when the apparently repentant Henry IV was kept waiting outside the castle for three days in the snow. It has always been a question as to who won when Henry was finally admitted, for Hildebrand had no wish to grant him absolution. In the end, Henry was able to regroup his forces and drive Hildebrand into exile.

COLLEGE OF CARDINALS: Composed of the priests and deacons of the principal churches of Rome, who in theory may be said to represent the people of Rome in the election of the Roman bishop. Few of the cardinals, to be sure, have discharged parish responsibilities in Rome, most of them having been occupied in the activities of the papal court or serving as prelates in distant lands, the parish duties being relegated to others.

his office as bishop of Rome, but this identification of authority with a particular office is nowhere to be found in the text. Lastly, assuming that Peter was given authority over the rest of the disciples, there is not the slightest basis for the notion that this power was to be transmitted to anyone else.

The oldest churches in Christendom, of course, were in the East, and there was never to be any acknowledgment among them of any superior authority to be exercised by the bishop of Rome, and when the imperial capital was transferred to Constantinople even the customary precedence in honor which had been accorded to the Roman church was to be challenged by the church of New Rome. Furthermore, in northern Europe, the non-Roman Christianity of Ireland was to be the dynamic and vital force in the conversion of the northern peoples. Only slowly over the centuries did the Roman church establish itself in western Europe as the symbol of orthodoxy which enjoyed a primacy of esteem and a presidency of honor. It was one thing to be in communion with Rome as the Anglican churches are today in communion with Canterbury; it was quite another matter to acknowledge Rome's superiority in jurisdiction. There was always a gap between the role which Rome claimed for itself and the authority which others were willing to acknowledge, and kings and princes were usually careful to safeguard the prerogatives of their own bishops. On occasion, of course, bargains were struck which were mutually advantageous.

2. *The Struggle for Independence*

The Christian church has never felt completely at ease in a subservient status to the state, and this was especially true of the church at Rome. During the century following Constantine's death, the disintegration of the imperial authority in Italy gave the church an opportunity to assert its independence. The earliest resistance to imperial control was led by Ambrose, bishop of Milan, at the close of the fourth century. In the sixth century, Gregory the Great succeeded in putting together a papal kingdom in the central portion of the Italian peninsula. Elsewhere in western Europe, the new chieftains and kings took bishops into their courts as officers of the state, and this status tended to be universalized when Charlemagne assumed the role of Constantine in a resurrected Roman Empire. It was not until the eleventh century that Hildebrand hammered out the theory and to a degree the fact of the independence of what by now had become the papal church. Even so, the notion that the bishop was the king's man did not completely disappear, and councils of the church continued to be called and presided over by kings and not by churchmen.

Hildebrand had come to power at the end of one of the most disastrous epochs in the history of the papal church. There had been ten bishops of Rome in the last decade of the ninth century. One of them had been strangled after he had dug up the corpse of his predecessor, stripped it of its pontifical garments, and ordered the body thrown in the Tiber. It was a time when petty local tyrants made and unmade popes at will. The first half of the eleventh century witnessed the scandalous rule of Benedict IX. Benedict had been consecrated bishop of Rome as a child of ten or twelve years, and he lived to behave like one of the most monstrous of the pagan emperors. He achieved the difficult feat of equaling the disgraceful record of two or three of the popes in the period immediately preceding the Reformation. In 1046, having tired of his papal office, Benedict put it up for sale. The purchaser, who took the name of Gregory VI, sought to effect some reforms, whereupon Benedict's family rebelled and reinstated Benedict in the Holy Office. Another faction had installed Sylvester III, so that there were three claimants to the papal honors. In response to an appeal to put an end to this disgraceful state of affairs, the Emperor Henry III intervened. Sylvester was imprisoned, Benedict's resignation was accepted, and Gregory VI was deposed and exiled. Henry insisted that only a foreign pope, protected by the emperor, could avoid the factional quarrels among the Roman populace which had debased the papacy. The next six popes were to be Germans, nominees of the emperor. They were able men, but none of them lived very long. The most distinguished was Leo IX, under whom Hildebrand became an influential figure.

Hildebrand had been a precocious child, educated in a Roman convent, and had entered the Benedictine order as a monk. At the age of twenty-three he had been enlisted to aid Gregory VI in his reform efforts, had organized an army, scattered Gregory's foes, and awed the local nobility. At this moment the emperor had intervened, and Hildebrand went into exile with his patron. Two years later he was back in Rome, to become the chief lieutenant of Leo IX as administrator of the papal states. Within ten years, this young monk who was not yet a priest had made himself master of the papacy, installing his own nominees in the chair of Peter, determining policies, and making the decisions. He much preferred to rule behind the scenes, but in 1073 he was pressured by a carefully organized demonstration into ascending the papal throne himself, becoming the bishop of Rome in name as well as in fact.

Hildebrand was dismayed by conditions which permitted the church to be a political football, and he sought to rectify this situation by making the church independent of political control. It was primarily with this end in view that he insisted upon a celibate clergy. If the church was to operate effectively in the face of external pressure, the clergy should be a disciplined force, free to obey their leader as implicity as soldiers carry out the orders of their commander. Above all, they must not have wives and families who could be held as hostages by political rulers. The investiture controversy which absorbed much of Hildebrand's attention was an attempt to deny to political rulers the right of appointing men to ecclesiastical office. And finally, in an effort to protect papal elections from outside interference, the right to elect the bishop of Rome was taken from the people of Rome and vested in the College of Cardinals. Hildebrand's aim was an independent and self-governing ecclesiastical structure.

3. *"The Intoxication of Victory"*

Independence was not all that Hildebrand sought. Arnold

Henry IV humbles himself at Canossa by kissing the foot of
Hildebrand (Gregory VII), while outside evidence of continued
resistance is seen.

Toynbee suggests that he became intoxicated by his success in winning the independence of the church and was led to overreach himself and claim the imperial power itself for the church. Others suggest that the course Hildebrand pursued was merely due to the fact that the church had lived too long in intimate association with the state to be content with its freedom alone.

This much is clear: the church in Rome had become infected by the imperial spirit and it longed for political power to fulfill its own imperial destiny. Thus not only did Hildebrand seek the freedom of the church to control its own life; he desired above all else that it should be supreme in political affairs as well. "The pope alone," he declared, "may use the imperial insignia; all persons shall kiss the foot of the pope alone; the pope has the power to depose emperors; his decree can be annulled by no one; he can annul the decrees of anyone; he can be judged by no one." "If a man consider the original of this great ecclesiastical dominion," said Thomas Hobbes, "he will easily perceive that the papacy is no other than the ghost of the deceased Roman Empire, sitting crowned upon the grave thereof. For so did the papacy start up on a sudden out of the ruins of that heathen power."

The actual temporal power exercised by Hildebrand and his successors has been greatly exaggerated. Rulers acquiesced to papal decrees when it was to their own advantage to do so, and ignored them when it was not. Thus William the Conqueror was easily persuaded to invade England with the papal blessing when Hildebrand wished to get rid of the archbishop of Canterbury. But, once having seized the English crown for himself, William refused to do homage for it to the pope, installed his own men as bishops, refused to permit them to make any appeal to Rome without his consent, and would not allow any papal bull or letter to be received in England or any papal legate to be admitted without his approval. On those occasions when a temporal ruler seemed to knuckle under to the papal will, it was often the result of more compelling pressures than papal displeasure. King John surrendered England to Innocent III and received it back as a fief in a desperate effort to save himself from the consequences of his own folly in alienating all possible support. The gamble, however, was unsuccessful, for he was forced to come to terms with the barons and signed the Magna Carta at Runnymede in 1215. Nor could Innocent help him by declaring the Great Charter null and void. The papal decree was flouted, excommunications were ignored, and the Charter became the symbol of English liberties. Even the Emperor Henry IV, who humbled himself before Hildebrand at Canossa, was not tamed, and it was Hildebrand who died in exile.

The barons of England force King John to sign the Great Charter, flouting the papal decree that it would be null and void.

While the papacy had difficulty making good its claims, it paid a stiff price for the attempt. In its endeavor to establish political authority over the peoples of Europe, the papal monarchy transformed itself into the image of its adversaries. Like the empire it sought to replace, the papacy engaged in diplomatic intrigue, maintained armies, and fought wars to achieve its ends. The popes became secular princes, living in ostentatious splendor and frequently spending as much as two-thirds of the income of the Holy See on their military budgets. The early Christians, James H. Nichols has commented, were willing to die rather than burn incense to Caesar; now much more than incense was being sacrificed to Caesarism. Those, like the Spiritual Franciscans among whom evangelical faith had been awakened by hearing the gospel, were often condemned to the stake or slain by the sword. For reasons Constantine would readily understand, Nichols has commented, the new papal Caesardom shed—according to the estimates of the historian Lecky—"more innocent blood than any other institution in human history."

QUESTIONS TO THINK ABOUT:

1. Apostolic succession is understood as a person-to-person continuity with the apostles through the laying on of hands in episcopal consecrations. Thus all Roman bishops are said to be in apostolic succession. How is this to be distinguished from the Petrine succession of the bishop of Rome?

2. The English Reformers insisted that the true mark of a bishop was not any outward succession but apostolic doctrine, a godly life, and pastoral labors. How would you evaluate the importance of these various guarantees?

3. Why has the freedom of the church to control and determine its own life been regarded as so important? How do you think a church may best secure and preserve its independence?

4. John Cotton suggested that for the church to exercise political authority is to make of the church a "monster." What are the dangers of the exercise of political authority by the church?

5. Hildebrand's goal was a Christian society. If you believe this goal to be valid but disagree with the methods by which he sought to achieve it, what would you suggest are the proper means for the church to employ in seeking to Christianize society?

SUGGESTIONS FOR FURTHER READING:

A brief but perceptive account of this ironic chapter in the history of the church is given by Arnold J. Toynbee, *A Study of History*, D. C. Somervell, ed. (Oxford University Press, 1947), pp. 349-59. Biographies of Hildebrand and Innocent III are to be found in J. T. McNeill, *Makers of Christianity* (Henry Holt and Co., 1935). Relevant documentary materials are reprinted in Henry Bettenson, *Documents of the Christian Church* (Oxford University Press, 1947), pp. 32-33, 111-116, 137-42, 157-58, 161-63.

v. Monks, Friars, and Reformers

Too often church life in the Middle Ages has been pictured solely in terms of the changing fortunes of the papacy, or in terms of the superstitions which had been domesticated in much of popular religion. The following pages, by emphasizing what J. H. Nichols has described as "the evangelical undertow" and by directing attention to one major movement for the outward reform of the church, should serve to rectify this distorted portrayal. Unfortunately, space does not permit a discussion of the remarkable penetration of culture by the Christian faith, of which the medieval cathedral and university stand as twin symbols.

FOR MANY CENTURIES and in many different ways the church was utilized as an instrument of worldly ambition, and something less than the full rigor of God's unconditional claim was laid upon the minds and hearts of its adherents. Nevertheless true faith was never extinguished, and it continued to show itself in recurring outbursts of evangelical life and in earnest efforts at reform.

1. *The Recurring Evangelical Witness*

The heroic demand of the Christian faith for a life of full devotion, obedience, self-sacrifice, and fellowship could never be completely obscured so long as the Christian story itself was not forgotten, and it found a recurring response in the monastic and lay revivals which kept welling up during the centuries between the age of Constantine and the Reformation.

The revivals of the monks and the friars were protests against the worldly living and secular concerns which disfigured the life of the church, but they had their source in the testimony

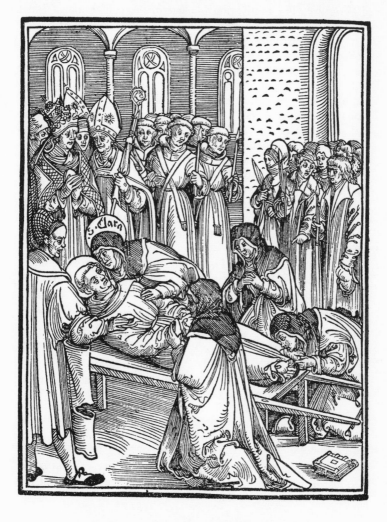

St. Francis of Assisi on his deathbed.
A sixteenth-century woodcut.

of Scripture. The motivation is clear in the confession of Basil of Caesarea: "When I had read the Gospel, and learned the best way of arriving at piety was to sell my goods and give them to the poor and to be no longer anxious about this life . . . , I wanted to find a brother who had chosen that path that we might pass through the short agitations of this life together." A similar experience had turned Jerome to the monastic life. At Antioch he had fallen ill, and in a vision he had seen himself dragged before the judgment seat. When he declared himself to be a Christian, the judge replied: "Thou liest, thou art a Ciceronian, not a Christian, 'for where thy treasure is there is thy heart also.'" For Francis of Assisi, it was also a gospel word—"provide neither gold, nor silver, nor brass in your purses, nor script for your journey, neither two coats, neither shoes, nor yet staves"—which had launched his little company upon an evangelical life of service and devotion.

The endeavor was to fashion a true Christian community in which the whole common life of devotion, labor, and possessions would be dedicated to Christian obedience and in which

---

BASIL OF CAESAREA: Noted as the father of Eastern monasticism. A strong supporter of Athanasius in the Arian controversy, he became bishop of Caesarea in 370.

PETER WALDO: A rich merchant of Lyons who renounced his wealth in 1176, taking literally Christ's command to "sell all thou hast, and give to the poor . . . , and come, follow me." His followers, many of whom became itinerant preachers of repentance, called themselves the "Poor in Spirit." Excommunicated in 1184, the members of the movement suffered a bloody repression.

FRIENDS OF GOD: An informal mystical brotherhood in southwest Germany and Switzerland, springing from the influence of two Dominican preachers—John Tauler (d. 1361) and Henry Suso (d. 1366).

BRETHREN OF THE COMMON LIFE: Communities for the cultivation of a practical piety, without permanent vows, in the

the responsibility of each member to minister in loving service was fully accepted. As has always been true of religious awakenings, the spiritual vitality of these movements would wane after a few generations. The communities were subject to the attrition of the world and over the years religious fervor would decline, discipline would grow lax, and evils would creep in. But then would come a movement of reform, recalling men to the earlier obedience.

If the evangelical fervor of monasticism had had a free course, it might have transformed the life of the church. Certainly the vows of chastity and poverty could not be universalized, but the devotion that was awakened could easily have been channeled into the concept of dedicated living in the world had it not presented a threat to the whole ecclesiastical structure. What actually occurred was that the impact of the monastic revivals was constantly deflected and its fervor isolated by developing the notion of a double way—two possible levels of life—for the Christian. Monasticism was but one way of life for a Christian—a way for the "religious" who took seriously Christ's counsels of perfection. Another way, it was

---

Netherlands and Germany, formed under the influence of Gerhard Groot (1340-1384), the author of the *Imitation of Christ,* which traditionally has been attributed to his disciple, Thomas à Kempis.

INQUISITION: Instrument for the detection and suppression of heresy, fashioned by Pope Gregory IX (1227-1241). Its proceedings were secret, the names of accusers were not disclosed, suspects were subjected to torture, and the property of those convicted was confiscated and shared with the lay authorities.

CONCILIARISTS: Advocates of governing the church by representative councils. Among the more prominent of the conciliarists were John of Paris (1265?-1306), a French Dominican; William of Ockham (d. 1349?), an English Franciscan, who studied at Oxford, taught at Paris, and was imprisoned by John XXII in 1328; and John Gerson (1363-1429), famed mystic and chancellor of the University of Paris, who was called the "soul" of the Council of Constance.

contended, had been provided for the vast majority of men. The ordinary person could know forgiveness by participating in the sacramental life of the church, without taking too seriously the claim of Christ upon his whole life.

The attempt to isolate the full Christian life behind monastery walls was never completely successful. The monks and especially the preaching orders of friars were not always willing to moderate and muffle the gospel when addressing themselves to the laity, and various "third orders" for those in the world who wished to give themselves to dedicated living came into existence. The notion of dedicated living also found expression in the lay mysticism of the Friends of God and in the semi-monastic communities of the Brethren of the Common Life. Sometimes the recurring outbursts of evangelical faith and life could not be diverted into these relatively safe channels. This was true of the movement led by Peter Waldo, the prototype of St. Francis. It was also true of the new spiritual life kindled by the preaching of John Wyclif and John Hus. Quite apart from these conspicuous figures and organized movements, there was always the influence of the preaching and example of countless numbers of humble parish priests who shepherded their flocks with true Christian devotion. Thus, throughout the darkest days of the church, men and women continued to be challenged to respond to the whole gospel with the whole life, and God's work of reconciling the world to himself did not lapse.

2. *"What Touches All Should Be Approved of All"*

At the beginning of the fourteenth century a notable group of university professors began to advocate the establishment of representative government in the church to replace the papal monarchy. Some of these men had become disillusioned as to the ability of the papacy to secure peace and unity among the peoples of western Europe; others were equally disturbed by the inability of the papacy to purge the church of manifest and glaring evils. Both groups were convinced that the papacy itself was part of the problem, and that the only remedy was the adoption of a system of parliamentary government for the church.

Quite obviously, with territories of its own to defend and armies to maintain, the papacy could scarcely be regarded as a disinterested party when it engaged in diplomatic maneuvers, and its supranational pretensions were apt to be viewed with a somewhat jaundiced eye. Indeed, there were many who felt that the papal ambitions served to increase rather than to diminish discord and strife. There was added cause for distrust of papal policy after 1309, for in that year the papal court was transferred from Rome to the French border and became in effect a French satellite. Among the other nations of Europe, papal emissaries were now regarded as agents of the French court in much the same way that the leaders of international Communism today are regarded as agents of Russia.

It seemed equally obvious to many that the papal court, with its extensive bureaucracy and vested interests, could never be expected to launch the needed attack upon abuses within the church, when such an attack would threaten its income and call into question its whole manner of life. The hopelessness of looking to the papacy for support in efforts for reform seemed clearly demonstrated by the policy which John XXII adopted toward the Spiritual Franciscans. Beginning in 1318, a systematic campaign was initiated to suppress and exterminate these humble and devoted followers of St. Francis. They were brought before the Inquisition and many of them were burned at the stake. Their sole offense was that, by insisting upon the faithful observance of the rule of their order, they were challenging papal authority, and this could not be tolerated.

As early as 1302, John of Paris was insisting that the papal powers were derived from the consent of the whole church and that the pope was accountable to and could be deposed by those who elected him. The events of 1309 and 1318 won added support for this contention. It now seemed clear beyond all possibility of doubt that the papacy was impotent to achieve either a general European concord or the reform of the church. Confronted by this impasse, the only alternative was to have

The Inquisition

a general council representing the church as a whole take the initiative and shoulder the burden of devising the necessary measures of reform.

The fundamental assumption of the Conciliarists was that the church was "the total society of the faithful," and the corollary to this was the principle drawn from the Code of Justinian that "what touches all must be approved of all." If the papacy would not and could not do what needed to be done, the whole church must be given an opportunity to act. As John Gerson was to point out, the creed does not say "I believe in the pope," but "I believe in the holy catholic Church." The proposal was to reduce the pope to the status of a constitutional monarch, with more dignity than power, and to vest actual authority in an elective assembly.

There was general agreement that the council should be truly representative, composed of both priests and laymen, chosen "from all the provinces or notable communities of the world." The method by which the representatives would be selected presented a perplexing problem. William of Ockham made the most specific suggestion. He would have representatives to a diocesan synod elected by a parish meeting, and the diocesan synod in turn would elect members of the general council. An even more difficult problem was to determine a method by which a council might be convened. The pope could scarcely be expected to summon a council which would undercut his own authority. The emperor was the most likely candidate, for there were ancient precedents of having councils convened by imperial decree. In actuality, however, the emperor was only one among several national monarchs, none of whom were willing to concede the right of initiative in such a matter to the emperor. There was even less likelihood of the French king's falling in line with such a proposal, so long as he was in a position to dominate the papal court at Avignon.

3. *Success and Failure*

The new situation created by the papal schism of 1378 was ultimately to resolve the problem as to how a council might be convened. Gregory XI had returned to Rome in 1377 and had died shortly thereafter. Urban VI was elected as his successor, but he offended the cardinals and they thereupon fled the city and elected Clement VII. There were now two popes, one at Rome and one at Avignon, and they proceeded to excommunicate each other. Not only did this create a scandalous situation; it was an expensive luxury, for two papal courts had now to be maintained. While Clement and his successors had the support of Spain, Scotland, Naples, and Sicily in addition to the support of France, the expense of maintaining the papal court at Avignon increasingly fell upon France alone. Ultimately France became weary of assuming this burden, and after thirty

Avignon, with its papal palace dominating the landscape

years of schism the other nations of Europe were ready to co-operate to bring it to an end. It was by general consent and with the co-operation of the cardinals of both papal courts, therefore, that a council assembled at Pisa in 1409 and proceeded to depose the two rival popes and elected a new one in their place. Unfortunately, the acquiescence of the two existing popes had not been secured and the result was simply to augment the confusion with a third pope.

Five years later the Council of Constance met. The three claimants to papal honors were now thoroughly discredited, but it took three years of negotiation and jockeying for position before the council was able to elect Martin V and to demonstrate in fact as well as in theory its superior authority in the life of the church. In order to prevent any future usurpation of the rights of the whole body of the faithful, a constitution was adopted which provided that another council should be held in five years, another in seven years, and one every ten years "forever after."

Councils did meet at Sienna in 1423 and at Basel in 1433, but the whole program was undermined by the man whom the Council of Constance had chosen as its chief administrative officer. Martin V broke his pledge to the council, repudiated his constitutional obligations, and sought to establish his own absolute authority in the church by negotiating separate concordats or bargains with each of the national rulers. By this means, the voice of the whole church was stifled and the papacy was permitted to pursue its heedless course unchecked.

4. *A Lesson Still to Be Learned*

In spite of the earnest effort to replace the papal monarchy with a representative assembly, the papacy was not diverted from the course which Hildebrand had charted for it. And in spite of the real faith and deep piety that was always to be found among both clergy and laity, the organized church itself remained largely untouched by the recurring outbursts of Christian devotion.

The Christian, as Stephen Neill has pointed out, is always called upon to judge the church "by what he learns of Christ and his purpose in the gospels." Confronted by a church that deliberately declared crusades for the extermination of whole peoples and subjected whole provinces to fire and slaughter, the Christian cannot escape the conviction that at some crucial point that church strayed from its allegiance to Christ.

Dante, looking back in the early years of the fourteenth century to discover the source of the ills which had overtaken the church, traced their beginning to the so-called Donation of Constantine, which served as the legal basis of the church's claim to temporal power. An eighth-century forgery long accepted as genuine, the Donation of Constantine purported to furnish documentary proof of the legend that Constantine, in gratitude for having been cured of leprosy by Pope Sylvester, shifted his base of operations to his new capital in the East and surrendered to the papacy undisputed political sovereignty in the West.

Although the document was spurious, Dante was essentially right in his analysis of the misfortunes which had overtaken the church. A church which seeks the pomp and splendor and power of Caesar has betrayed its Lord no less than the church which exists only as an appendage to Caesar's throne, blessing and sanctifying the policies of the ruler in return for protection and favor. In both instances, from a means of mediating the redemption offered in Christ, the church itself becomes urgently in need of the redemption it claims to possess. The church must then learn again the lesson that not even the society of Christ can escape the necessity for repentance and humble submission to the One whose kingdom can never be established by the might and power of men. In Stephen Neill's vivid words, so unfaithful to God's rule of gentleness and grace had the church become as to make inevitable such a judgment upon it as had been pronounced by the prophets of former times against unfaithful Israel of old.

QUESTIONS TO THINK ABOUT:

1. Various efforts have been made to trace a "succession" in the church. Sometimes a succession of persons has been emphasized, sometimes a succession of office, sometimes a succession of organization. Do you regard any of these as adequate? What would you regard as the true succession?

2. The Protestant Reformers were to insist that what the New Testament said it said to all, that every man is called upon to respond with full devotion wherever he is and in whatever occupation he pursues. Every man is called to be a monk all his life, was the vivid way in which Sebastian Franck put it. But is there not something to be said for a double standard for Christians on the basis that not everyone can be expected to be a model Christian?

3. It has been said that every great forward movement in the church has been the consequence of someone's rediscovering the Christ of the Scriptures. Do you think that this is true?

4. Do you think that God's truth is more adequately represented by the whole company of the faithful rather than by any segment

of the church? Why? What should the respective roles of the clergy and the laity be in the preservation of God's truth in the church?

5. What makes the reform of the church so difficult?

SUGGESTIONS FOR FURTHER READING:

Roland H. Bainton's chapter, "The Ministry in the Middle Ages," in H. Richard Niebuhr, ed., *The Ministry in Historical Perspectives* (Harper & Brothers, 1956), describes the varied church life of the period. Representative writings of the Conciliarists are reprinted in Vol. XIV of the *Library of Christian Classics,* Matthew Spinka, ed., *Advocates of Reform* (Westminster Press, 1953). The spirit of monasticism is reflected in the letters of Jerome which are reprinted in Vol. V of the same series, S. L. Greenslade, ed., *Early Latin Theology* (Westminster Press, 1956). Insight into the spirit of Francis' ministry of reconciliation may best be gained from the legends incorporated in *The Little Flowers of St. Francis,* a slender volume which has been republished many times.

VI. The Church Recovers Its Life

The Protestant Reformation was made possible by many external factors—political, economic, cultural. This fact has sometimes been allowed to obscure the more important fact that the Reformation was primarily a religious movement, finding its basic orientation and dynamic in a rediscovery of the gospel. The following discussion seeks to identify the focal point of religious concern and to spell out its implications for the life of the church.

SIX YEARS AFTER Martin Luther nailed his Ninety-five Theses to the door of the Castle Church in Wittenberg, an anxious mother sent a little wax lamb marked *Agnus Dei* to her son who was studying at Wittenberg, in the hope that it would protect him from harm. The son's reply has been preserved and reads as follows:

Dear Mother:
You should not be upset over Dr. Martin Luther's teaching, nor worried about me. . . . I am grateful to you for sending me the little wax *Agnus Dei* to protect me against being shot, cut, and from falling, but honestly it won't do me any good. I cannot set my faith on it because God's Word teaches me to trust only in Jesus Christ. I am sending it back. We'll try it out on this letter and see whether it is protected from tampering. I don't thank you one bit less, but I pray God that you won't believe any more in sacred salt and holy water and all this devil's tomfoolery. I hope you won't give the wax lamb to my brother. And dearest mother, I hope father will let me stay longer in Wittenberg. Read Dr. Martin Luther's New Testament. It is on sale at Leipzig. I am going to buy a brown hat. . . . Love to my dear father and brothers and sisters.

The Castle Church at Wittenberg

"God's Word teaches me to trust only in Jesus Christ." This was the great word of the Protestant Reformation, and it was in terms of this insistence that a person must place his trust in Christ alone that the church was to recover the life that is to be found only in the Church.

1. *The Need of the Church to Recover Its Life*

A brief catalogue of the men who occupied the papal throne in the years immediately preceding the Reformation is sufficient to illustrate the extent to which the life of the church had been disfigured. Pius II, Paul II, and Sixtus IV were splendor-loving princes, of whom little that is kind can be said. Innocent VIII summarized his conception of the Holy Office with his cynical quip that "God does not wish the death of a sinner but that

he should live and pay." Alexander VI was a disreputable
scoundrel who shrank from no crime, for to him nothing was
sacred. When he died, a report circulated among the people
of Rome that "the devil was seen standing beside his bed ready
to carry his soul down to hell." Leo X, who occupied the See
of Peter at the time the Reformation began, has been described
as the best of the Renaissance popes, but the best was none
too good. A son of Lorenzo the Magnificent, Leo had been
ordained a priest at the age of seven and had become a cardinal
at the age of thirteen. His comment at the time of his corona-
tion—"Let us enjoy the papacy, since God has given it to us"
—aptly expressed his program. He sought to make life one
long carnival, squandering the income of the Holy See and being
forced by his extravagance to borrow to the limit of his credit.
Of Leo, a Roman Catholic historian has commented: "Leo
would have been a perfect pope, if he had combined with his
other good qualities, a moderate knowledge of religion and a
greater inclination to piety, for neither of which he showed
much concern."

NINETY-FIVE THESES: Topics for academic debate, dealing
with indulgences, posted by Luther on October 31, 1517. Osten-
sibly noncommittal, they actually called in question the whole structure of the church as understood and defended by the papacy.

PROTESTANT REFORMATION: The basic issues were defined
by Luther in the three great manifestoes of 1520, and the Reformation became firmly established in much of Germany during the next
few years. The penetration of Scandinavia occurred during the
1530's. The Swiss Reformation was inaugurated at Zurich by
Huldreich Zwingli in 1522, but it was not until 1536 that John
Calvin began his activity at Geneva and published his *Institutes
of the Christian Religion*. In England the break with Rome was
completed in 1534, although the religious settlement was not
stabilized until the accession of Elizabeth in 1558. The Scottish
Reformation occurred in 1560 under the leadership of John Knox,
and in the Netherlands William of Orange accepted the Reformed
faith in 1573.

There was something fundamentally wrong with an understanding of the Christian faith which could tolerate, excuse, and even foster such scandalous conditions in the life of the church. This was a point clearly recognized by all the Reformers. The struggle in which he was engaged, Martin Luther insisted, was over faith and not practice, over doctrine and not morals. The scandals and abuses which plagued the life of the church were symptoms of a basic misunderstanding and misinterpretation of the Christian faith. Even if the morals were to be amended, Luther contended, the faith would still be unsound and the fundamental defect would remain.

The church had become an institution which could be utilized by men for purposes quite foreign to the spirit of Christ, because God's work of reconciling the world to himself had come to be regarded as being restricted to the ceremonies performed by the clergy. Outside the rites of the church—controlled and administered by the clergy—there was thought to be no salvation. The clergy could either grant or withhold divine grace. Thus the concept of the church as the people of God had

LORENZO THE MAGNIFICENT: The father of Leo X was a member of the immensely wealthy Medici family. He had succeeded his father as virtual ruler of Florence in 1469 and had ushered in the most brilliant age in Florentine history by his lavish support of Renaissance scholars and artists.

JOHANN TETZEL: A Dominican employed by Albrecht of Brandenburg to sell indulgences, with the proceeds being divided with Leo X. Tetzel's merchandising zeal had provoked Luther to post the Ninety-five Theses.

HUGH LATIMER AND NICHOLAS RIDLEY: English Reformers who were burned at the stake by Queen Mary (1553-1558) on October 16, 1555.

JOHN FOXE: An English Reformer who was in exile at Strassburg during the reign of Queen Mary. His history of Christian martyrs was published in Latin at Basel in 1559. The first of the many English editions was published in 1563.

been displaced by what has not unjustly been described as a "clerical closed shop" which could pressure both the humble and the mighty to do its bidding with the threat of eternal damnation.

By the end of the Middle Ages the clergy had at their disposal a host of devices by which the docile and obedient could gain merit in the eyes of God, and they claimed the additional power to grant actual dispensations to sin as well as indulgences

The hawking of indulgences

which would permit the foresighted to escape penalties which they normally might be expected to suffer. Ultimately, even the fate of the dead in purgatory was brought within the scope of clerical control by the suggestion that the period of torment might be reduced or even canceled upon recommendation by the proper authorities. When Tetzel, the Dominican friar, hawked the goods of the church with the couplet,

> As soon as the coin in the coffer rings,
> The soul from purgatory springs,

he was making an unduly extravagant claim, but while the reasonable presumption of the moderates that God would not turn a deaf ear to the recommendation of his ecclesiastical lieutenants may have been more defensible in theory, it scarcely represented a significant difference in actual practice.

2. *The Rediscovery of the Church as the People of God*

When the student at Wittenberg wrote to his mother that "God's Word teaches us to trust only in Jesus Christ," he was voicing a belief that undercut the whole system of clerical control. Reconciliation with God, he was saying, is not determined by any priest. God can be put under obligation and coerced by no man. The forgiveness he extends is an act of pure grace, merited by no one. It is a gift, freely offered to all who respond in trust to God's invitation and promise. This was the fundamental theme of all the Reformers.

The fresh recognition by the Reformers of the true nature of the Christian faith led them to discover again the true nature of the Church as a people, God's people, the whole body of the faithful. Luther, in fact, did not like to use the word "church," for it seemed to him to convey no clear meaning. He much preferred to give the word "ecclesia" a more precise translation by utilizing such words as "community," "congregation," "assembly," "crowd," "people." The Church is a people, a fellowship, a communion of persons who have been related to their fellow believers and to all men in the spirit of faith and love awakened in them by God's Word. The Church is not to be thought of apart from Christ, nor is Christ to be thought of apart from the Church. It is his Body—the community in which and through which Christ becomes visible to the world.

3. *Three Major Convictions*

On the basis of this understanding of the nature of the Church, the Reformers arrived at three major convictions—

convictions that spelled the end of clerical tyranny and control.

First of all, *the true Church*—the company of all the faithful—*must never be confused or equated with a particular, historical ecclesiastical institution*. The true Church is not an institution and it is circumscribed by no institutional boundaries. It exists wherever there is faith. The place of God may have been usurped and people may have been misled by papal claims, but the Church had not ceased to exist. "Where was your faith before Luther?" a French peasant woman is reported to have been asked by a devout and kindly priest. "In the hearts of people like you," was her immediate response. Wherever the Bible with its witness to Christ has been preserved, faith may be awakened; and wherever faith has been awakened, there Christ is to be found; and wherever Christ is to be found, there is the Church.

In the second place, *this understanding of the nature of the Church meant that men could not place their reliance upon any external relationship to an institution*. One does not become a Christian by joining a church, partaking of its sacraments, performing its rites, or submitting to its authority. Faith to be valid must be personal. The decisive event occurs within the secrecy of one's own soul. Said a sixteenth-century Anglican divine: "It is not enough for you to say that you believe as the church of the elect and chosen of God doth believe, unless you know and feel in your hearts what thing it is that the church believeth. Your faith must not be grounded upon any other man's faith. Believe not the doctrine because I or any other preacher doth preach it unto you, but believe it to be true because your own faith doth assure you it to be true."

Lastly, *this conception of the Church as a people meant that the vocation of the priesthood,* far from being the monopoly of a special caste within the church, *was the common possession of all Christians*. "The consequence of being one with Christ," said Luther, "is that we are also one among ourselves." Every Christian is called to be a priest, a mediator of Christ, an intercessor for his neighbor, a witness to the gospel, a Christ to his fellows. All Christians, declared Luther, "are worthy to appear before God, to pray for others, to teach others mutually the things that are of God . . . , and each should become to the other a sort of Christ, so that we may be mutually Christs, and that the same Christ may be in all of us."

This did not mean that there was to be no stated or public ministry in the church. Not every person could be expected to have either the talent or the training to interpret difficult points of Scripture adequately, nor the time to assume responsibility for the general pastoral care of the congregation. Furthermore, for the sake of order in the church, specific duties had to be assigned; and quite obviously, if there was to be order, no one could be permitted to do that which belonged to all without the consent of all. A stated ministry was as necessary as it had been in the days of the early church, but it was a ministry defined in terms of function rather than in terms of a unique status before God. The minister acted for the people only in a *representative* capacity. On all fundamental issues, as J. H. Nichols has pointed out, he was to be regarded as "only another 'believer' of the same rank with the 'ministers' in the pews." This was not to minimize the importance of the clergy within the Christian community, but it did deny them any monopoly of the means of God's grace. The Christ that is offered in the preaching of the Word and in the Supper of the Lord is the same Christ that is made available by all believers through the testimony of their lives.

The simple affirmation of "trust in Christ alone" touched the very heart of the church's life, and, as its implications were pursued, the church began to recover its true life as a people— a fellowship of believers—all of whom were called to be priests, chosen ministers of God, the servants in Christ of their fellow men.

4.   *"Such a Candle as by God's Grace Shall Never Be Put Out"*

When news of the tumult occasioned by Luther's Ninety-five Theses reached Rome, Leo X dismissed it as a mere squabble among monks, commenting: "Luther is a drunken German. He will think differently when he is sober." By 1520, however, it had become apparent that Luther's teaching threatened to topple the whole structure of clerical and papal control. Alarmed at last, Leo drafted a sentence of excommunication in the form of a call to arms: "Arise, O Lord, and judge thy cause. A wild boar has invaded thy vineyard. . . . We can no longer suffer the serpent to creep through the field of the Lord." The edict placing Luther under the ban of the Empire was equally violent: "This devil in the habit of a monk has brought together ancient errors into one stinking puddle and invented new ones. He denies the power of the keys. . . . His teaching makes for rebellion, division, war, murder, robbery, arson, and the collapse of Christendom. He lives the life of a beast. . . . No one is to harbor him. His followers also are to be condemned. His books are to be eradicated from the memory of man."

Luther acknowledged that it was "hard to dissent from all the pontiffs and princes," but there was no other way. "The faith and the Church are at stake." When asked whether he would come to the Imperial Diet where he had been summoned to appear, he replied: "I will go even if I am too sick to stand on my feet. . . . If violence is used, as well it may be, I commend my cause to God. . . . If he will not save me, my head is worth nothing compared with Christ. This is no time to think of safety. I must take care that the gospel is not brought into contempt by our fear to confess and seal our teaching with our blood." To Melanchthon, Luther wrote: "My dear brother, if I do not come back, if my enemies put me to death, you will go on teaching and standing fast in the truth; if you live my death will matter little."

A new age of the martyrs had dawned. "Trust in Christ alone" could mean and did mean death for many, and for his sake they were willing to die. Ever faithful to the truth he had received, Luther stood before the emperor and in response to the demand that he recant on penalty of death replied: "Since your majesty and your lordships desire a plain answer, I will give you one. . . . Unless I am convinced by Scripture and plain reason . . . , I cannot and will not recant anything, for to go against conscience is neither right nor safe. God help me. Amen." Another report added the words that have become immortal as the symbol of Luther's spirit: "Here I stand, I can do no other."

Luther was spared, spirited away by his friends, but others were not. Throughout Europe the fires were being kindled. In England, when Bishops Ridley and Latimer were being bound

Hugh Latimer and Nicholas Ridley being burned at the stake, while a contemptuous sermon is preached on the text: "Though I give my body to be burned and have not love, it profiteth me nothing."

to the stake, Latimer said to his friend: "Be of good cheer, Master Ridley, and play the man, for we shall this day light such a candle in England as I trust by God's grace shall never be put out."

The roll of those martyred is a long one, and the memory of

their faithfulness even to death was preserved by John Foxe in his *Book of Martyrs*—a volume which for three centuries to come was to have a place of honor beside the Bible in all Protestant homes. Some of those who traveled the steep ascent to heaven by a martyr's death were distinguished churchmen, but most were humble obscure folk whose only fault was that they had been taught by God's Word to trust in Christ alone. Neither fire nor sword, however, availed to put out the light of God's truth, and the life of the Church as God's people, which had been so long obscured and disfigured, was recovered.

QUESTIONS TO THINK ABOUT:

1. What other implications are there in the affirmation that we must place our trust in Christ alone? To what extent, from day to day, are we tempted to place our trust in ourselves rather than in Christ?

2. It has been suggested that the deplorable conditions which infected the papacy are evidence of its divine origin and character, for otherwise it would never have been able to survive them. How would you respond to this contention?

3. What do you conceive the role of the minister to be? On what grounds are certain functions restricted only to those who are ordained?

4. What is the meaning of the "priesthood of all believers"? Can it be said that every believer is his own priest?

5. Monasticism was condemned partly on the basis of "the universality of the Christian vocation." What is the meaning of this doctrine?

SUGGESTIONS FOR FURTHER READING:

A brief and incisive account of the Reformation is given by E. Harris Harbison, *The Age of the Reformation* (Cornell University Press, 1955). Perceptive analyses of various facets of the Reformation are to be found in Wilhelm Pauck, *The Heritage of the Reformation* (Beacon Press, 1950). Among the writings which most clearly reflect Luther's thinking concerning the church are his *Address to the Christian Nobility of the German Nation* (1520), *Treatise on Good Works* (1520), *Christian Liberty* (1520), *The Right and Power of a Christian Congregation to Call and Dismiss Preachers* (1523), and *On the Councils and the Churches* (1539).

VII. The Reformation Churches

A curious feature of the Reformation is the fact that so little thought was given to the question of the outward organization and government of the church. This neglect, however, is not surprising when we remember that fundamental issues of faith had absorbed the attention of the Reformers and that the struggle with Rome exhausted their energies. While not surprising, the failure to grapple seriously with the problem of ecclesiastical construction meant that the Reformation was essentially incomplete. Among the tasks that were left to the future were the determination of the role of the people in the life of the church by virtue of their common priesthood, the safeguarding by appropriate guarantees of the independence of the church, and the issues presented by religious diversity.

CLASSICAL PROTESTANTISM IS represented by three major ecclesiastical traditions: Lutheran, Anglican, Reformed-Presbyterian. The other major Protestant bodies—Congregationalists, Baptists, Methodists, Disciples—are post-Reformation in origin. These latter bodies were not the product of any marked theological dissent. They arose as the result of differences of opinion on the implications for church order or polity of the basic theological convictions of the Reformers.

The Reformation, as we have seen, had re-emphasized the true nature of the Church as the people of God and had insisted that one's trust must be placed in Christ alone rather than in any ecclesiastical institution or clerical caste. Even at the time of the Reformation, however, not everyone was entirely happy with the steps that were taken to remodel the structure of organized church life so that it might more adequately express the true community to be found in Christ. Dissatisfaction at this point gave rise to the so-called left-wing movements of reform on the Continent, but of far greater future importance was the impetus it gave in England to the development of Puritanism. The issue was stated clearly by the "Dissenting Brethren" of the Westminster Assembly in *An Apologetical Narration* which they issued in 1643. They confessed that they regarded the Reformers with great reverence and esteem, yet they "could not but suppose" that the Reformers might not have perceived clearly "all things about worship and government, their intentions being most spent . . . upon the reformation in doctrine, in which they had a most happy hand."

Martin Luther

1. *The Lutheran Churches*

There is something to be said for the contention that Luther had not given sufficient attention to the task of ordering the outward life of the Church. The insistence that the Church was a people rather than an ecclesiastical institution was used effectively by Luther in criticizing Roman clericalism, but he failed to apply this insistence constructively when he was confronted by the task of replacing the old church order with new ecclesiastical arrangements more in keeping with his conception of the Church.

Luther believed that a valid church order must be of such a character as to make it possible (1) for the Word of God to be freely preached and (2) for the members of the Christian congregations to assume the responsibilities of their common priesthood. He further believed that "the task of establishing a true church order in the world belonged to the 'Christian people' themselves." Thus we find Luther suggesting that the Christian believers should have the right to determine their own officers, call their own pastors, and judge what constituted true preaching. Luther's most difficult problem was to determine who among the general populace could reasonably be regarded as Christian believers and hence could be entrusted with the responsibilities of church life. Before he had really faced this problem, the pressure of events forced his hand and compelled him to improvise in terms of the necessities of the immediate situation.

The initial consequence of the Lutheran critique of the established church order was confusion and chaos. This was notably true in terms of ecclesiastical property. What was to become of the deserted monastic cloisters and their endowments? It was equally true in terms of worship. Varied patterns of liturgical reform were being introduced in each village, frequently with little attention being paid to decency and decorum. What of the ministry itself? Should there be a stated ministry at all? Could not any layman officiate at public worship? And how was provision to be made for religious instruction? Furthermore, differences of doctrine were appearing. Complicating the situation was the fact that the activity of extremists was serving to discredit the movement in the eyes of many and gave some color to the charge that society itself was being subverted. Everywhere there was uncertainty, unrest, and disorder.

It seemed obvious enough that someone must take the initiative in dealing with these practical problems and in restoring some semblance of order to church life. Since the confusion and disorder were disturbing wide areas, the problems could scarcely be settled on a parish basis. Ideally the bishops should have taken the initiative, but they had not accepted the Reformation. The alternative was to have superintendents who would provide the necessary leadership. But who was to create this office? How were they to be chosen? If by the churches, who was to call them together? On the spur of the moment, no one appeared better qualified than the princes. The responsibility

---

WESTMINSTER ASSEMBLY OF DIVINES: Summoned by the English Parliament in 1643, during the Puritan Revolution, to advise the Parliament with regard to the adoption of a new form of church government to replace the abolished episcopacy. Among the documents drafted by the Assembly were the Confession of Faith, and the Larger and Smaller Catechisms. These so-called Westminster Standards were later adopted by the Church of Scotland and to varying degrees by the American Presbyterians, Congregationalists, and Baptists.

DISSENTING BRETHREN: A minority group within the Westminster Assembly, who advocated a congregational rather than a presbyterian form of government for the Church of England.

THOMAS CRANMER: Archbishop of Canterbury (1532-1556). Cranmer was instrumental in enabling Henry VIII to overthrow the Papal supremacy in England. His thinking grew more and more Protestant and he was degraded and forced to recant during the reign of Mary Tudor. But he renounced his recantation before dying at the stake in 1556. His enduring contribution was made as chief architect of the Prayer Books on which *The Book of Common Prayer* is based.

for reordering church life belonged, by virtue of their common priesthood, to the laity; and the princes, by virtue of their position, were the actual leaders among the laity. Should not the princes, therefore, who had been "risking not only their kingdoms but their lives by espousing the Lutheran gospel in defiance of the imperial decree," take the initiative on behalf of their fellow priests? Thus it was that Luther turned to the princes as "emergency bishops" and called upon them to institute procedures for orderly church life.

Unfortunately, what Luther regarded as a temporary expedient became a permanent system. Power once assumed is not readily surrendered, and the princes took over full control of the church. So long as the prince was a Christian, or even merely indifferent, the arrangement was tolerable, for it did not overtly prevent the Word of God from being freely preached. In the longer perspective, however, the failure to erect any

---

JOHN WHITGIFT: Bishop of Worcester (1577-1583), and archbishop of Canterbury (1583-1604). Theologically a stanch Calvinist, Whitgift was a leading defender of the Elizabethan religious settlement.

JOHN JEWEL: A Protestant exile under Mary Tudor, Jewel became bishop of Salisbury on the accession of Elizabeth. He and Richard Hooker became the most noted apologists of official Anglicanism.

ANDREW MELVILLE: With the death of John Knox in 1572, Melville returned from a teaching post in Geneva to become the leader of Scottish Presbyterianism. Melville was of the same sturdy spirit as Knox and did not hesitate to remind the monarch of his duty to God, calling James I on one occasion "God's silly vassal." The last years of his life were spent in exile among the French Protestants.

PATRON: A person possessing the right of patronage, i.e., the right to nominate or appoint a clergyman to an ecclesiastical office. The right of patronage usually was acquired by the person who built a church at his own expense, and it was passed on to his heirs as a property right.

constitutional safeguards to protect the independence of the church was to have disastrous consequences. A more immediate unhappy consequence was the fact that, within the limits of state control, the church became a clerically dominated institution. The clergy, being appointed by and responsible to the prince, took charge and left to the people a purely passive role. Thus there was no provision for any real congregational life, and the idea of a priesthood of believers actually expressing itself through the exercise of responsibility by local congregations remained only as a reminder of what might have been.

2.   *The Church of England*

In England the outcome of the Reformation was much the same. The initiative from the very beginning was taken by the king, and no Tudor or Stuart was ever willing to relinquish power voluntarily. There was this significant difference: the English monarchs were able to command the co-operation of the majority of the bishops, and, as a consequence, the outward structure of the church—with its dioceses and parishes, its bishops and parish clergy—was largely left untouched. The church, however, retained no power to order its own life. The bishops did not possess the right to appoint the clergy they were expected to govern nor to determine what sort of men they should be. And once a man was inducted into a parish, the bishop had no powers to discipline him. Ultimately when a later generation of bishops with royal support began to impose a measure of conformity upon the clergy, they were able to do so only by making use of nonecclesiastical courts and by drawing upon the reserved powers of the crown. The church itself had no independent authority of its own. For a time, to be sure, the meeting of convocation kept alive the appearance of a self-governing church, but eventually even this fiction was surrendered.

The fundamental article of the Church of England as established by law was the Royal Supremacy, and it was on this basis that the peculiarities of the English Reformation were defended. Thomas Cranmer gave classic expression, as early as

1540, to belief in the authority of the "Godly Prince": "All Christian Princes have committed unto them immediately of God, the whole cure of all their subjects, as well concerning the administration of God's word for the cure of souls, as concerning the ministration of things political, and civil governance." Those who were thrust into the difficult position of

Thomas Cranmer

being apologists for the king's or queen's religion had first to assert that "one certain form or kind of external government [of the church] perpetually to be observed is nowhere in the scripture prescribed." They could then assert, as Whitgift did, that the king, to whom "God hath given the chief government of his church," can determine and ordain "what is most convenient." Or, as John Jewel put it, "it is lawful for a godly prince to command bishops and priests, to make laws and orders for the church, to redress the abuses of the sacraments, to allege the scriptures, to threaten and punish bishops and priests, if they offend." Thus the determining theological conviction for the English church was neither the conception of the Church as the people of God nor the doctrine of the priesthood of believers, but the conception of divine-right monarchy, with the ultimate authority in the church being concentrated in the hands of the king.

The restlessness of many of the English clergy and people is easy to understand. It is difficult to adjust the consciences of earnest Christians to the whim of the monarch, and the apologists had not emphasized Luther's confidence in the power of the Word alone to triumph over all obstacles which had served to ease consciences in Lutheran lands. As disturbing to many as the lack of responsible and independent government in the church was the absence of any real congregational life. Intermittently random attempts would be made to provide for a responsible exercise of the common priesthood in the life of the church, such as the establishment of a parish lectureship, but no permanent constitutional provisions along this line were achieved prior to the parish councils of the twentieth century.

3. *The Reformed-Presbyterian Churches*

Unlike Lutheranism and Anglicanism, the church structure fashioned within the Reformed or Presbyterian tradition provided for representative self-government and in various ways sought to foster a full congregational life. This was partly due

John Calvin

to the fact that John Calvin, the major architect of the Reformed polity, constructed his constitution for the church within the more democratic context of Geneva, and thus it was much easier to give the people a voice in the affairs of the church. The decisive issue as to whether the Reformed churches should embrace the whole community or be composed only of believers, however, was not frankly faced. In many areas beyond Geneva, as in France and Hungary, the minority status of the Reformed churches provided an automatic sifting of members, and hence in these areas the question was purely academic. In Geneva a different situation prevailed, for the city itself became a select community. Those who refused to make their peace with the church were banished from the city, and this exodus was paralleled by an influx of refugees from outside who were fully committed to the program of reform. No less than six thousand of these refugees were admitted to a city whose original population was thirteen thousand. "Thus by the expulsion of dissenters and the inclusion of the conformists, Geneva became a city of the saints. . . . None but the convinced belonged to the church, but everyone in Geneva belonged to the church because those who did not left the town."

The leaders of the Reformation in Scotland were sons of Geneva. They had been schooled in exile, and they had learned by stern experience the lesson that the integrity of the church could be maintained only if its freedom to govern itself was preserved. It has been said of these Scottish leaders that they feared God so much that they could not fear any man. John Knox had spent eighteen months in the French galleys and remained undaunted. Andrew Melville was of the same sturdy spirit. When threatened with hanging if he did not stop preaching, Melville replied: "Tush, sir, threaten your courtiers after that fashion. It is all the same to me whether I rot in the air or the ground."

The Scottish Reformation dates from the adoption of a Protestant Confession of Faith by the Scottish Parliament in 1560, but the actual work of reforming the church was carried through by a General Assembly which met without royal war-

John Knox

rant or parliamentary sanction. Its authority to regulate its own ecclesiastical affairs, it was insisted, was derived directly from Christ. "Right religion," Knox informed Queen Mary, "takes neither origin nor authority from worldly princes but from the eternal God alone," and therefore subjects must not "frame their religion according to the appetite of their princes." It was with this fundamental point in mind that Knox declared that, if you "take from us the freedom of assemblies," you "take from us the gospel." For without free assemblies, he continued, "how shall good order and unity in doctrine be kept?"

The basic constitution of the Scottish church, which conferred upon it the right of self-government, was confirmed by Parliament and received the royal assent in 1567. The local unit of government was to be in the church session, from which appeal could be made to a regional synod, and from the synod an appeal could be carried to the General Assembly. From the judgment of the General Assembly there was to be no further appeal, neither to the king nor to the Parliament. All these bodies were to be composed of both clerical and lay representatives.

Three issues were left unresolved. First of all, the right of patrons to nominate the minister to be installed in a particular parish was not abrogated, and it was to lead to bitter strife when unwanted ministers were intruded by this means upon unwilling congregations. In the second place, while some sifting of membership for purposes of church government was made possible by disciplinary procedures, the church was a national church embracing the total community. Such an arrangement was tolerable in a city of saints such as Geneva, and it was to be tolerable for several generations in the peculiar Scottish situation. The Reformation was the occasion for a popular uprising against the French power and influence in Scottish life, and the Reformed church became the symbol of national unity. Thus the Scottish people as a whole became loyal sons of the church with a firm allegiance to its standards. Lastly, while the constitution of the church provided for self-government, the church was established by law. This fact made plausible the argument that what the state had created the state could alter, and bloody battles were to be fought as a result of attempts by the civil power to impose its will upon the church.

The obvious conclusion to be drawn from this survey of the three major expressions of classical Protestantism is that the Reformation was essentially incomplete. With regard to the outward ordering of the life of the church, much was left by the Reformers for future generations to do. There were still lessons to be learned.

QUESTIONS TO THINK ABOUT:

1. What are the ways in which Christians may exercise responsibility in the life of the church?

2. If the laity are to participate in the government of the church, what is the peril of extending the privileges of church membership to the total community?

3. How important do you believe it to be for the church to be self-governing and independent?

4. Some people suggest that the dependence of the minister upon voluntary support seriously compromises his freedom as a minister

of Christ, for he then becomes the prisoner of the prejudices of his congregation. How valid do you regard this contention? What are the alternative means of ministerial support? Are there dangers in a dependence upon the state or endowments for the support of the ministry?

SUGGESTIONS FOR FURTHER READING:

The several Reformation traditions are discussed with clarity and insight by Roland H. Bainton, *The Reformation of the Sixteenth Century* (Beacon Press, 1952), and subsequent developments are briefly described by J. H. Nichols, *History of Christianity, 1650-1950* (Ronald Press, 1956), pp. 41-67. A detailed account of Anglican views of the ministry is provided by Norman Sykes, *Old Priest and New Presbyter* (Cambridge University Press, 1956), and a selection from Richard Hooker's *Laws of Ecclesiastical Polity* is reprinted in H. E. Fosdick, *Great Voices of the Reformation* (Random House, 1952). A systematic statement of Calvin's views concerning the church is to be found in Book IV of his *Institutes of the Christian Religion*. Three other documents—*Articles Concerning the Organization of the Church* (1537), *Reply to Sadolet* (1539), and *Ecclesiastical Ordinances* (1541)—are reprinted in Vol. XII of the *Library of Christian Classics*.

VIII. The Post-Reformation Churches

The Reformation left several issues unsettled. One obvious problem was the age-old question of the freedom and independence of the church. Most of the Reformation churches lost the right to govern themselves and became captives of the civil authorities, and even in Geneva and Scotland a satisfactory solution had not been found. A closely allied problem was that of the place of the laity in the life of the church, and this problem was complicated by yet a third, which stemmed from the hesitancy of the Reformers to surrender the notion that every member of society should be included within the membership of the church. But if this position was to be maintained, how could the people of a parish —including both believers and unbelievers, the sincere and the indifferent, the devout and the scoffer—be safely entrusted with any real responsibility for the life of the church? When these problems were faced and solutions attempted, other problems arose, for one result was the formation of new Protestant denominations.

THE FOUR MAJOR post-Reformation Protestant bodies are the Congregationalists, the Baptists, the Methodists, and the Disciples or "Christians." All had their origin in the English-speaking world, the first three in England itself and the last in the United States. The Congregationalists and the Baptists arose within seventeenth-century English Puritanism, while the Methodists and Disciples were products of the Evangelical Revival of the eighteenth and nineteenth centuries. It is especially important to understand the concerns which brought these four denominations into existence, for the two movements which produced them exerted a decisive influence upon all the churches of the English-speaking world.

1. *Congregationalists and Baptists*

The Elizabethan religious settlement which gave outward form to the Church of England was a compromise settlement, partly because Elizabeth's own tastes and inclinations were conservative, while those of the men upon whom she had to depend for leadership in the church were strongly Protestant. Political considerations were even more important. Elizabeth had come to the throne in 1558 after a decade when the threat of open revolt was never absent, and she was determined to make her position secure by building as broad a base of support as possible by offending as few people as possible. The church which was the product of this concern was not entirely satisfactory to anyone, and its chief merit at the moment was the fact that it was not unduly offensive to anyone.

There were, nevertheless, a number of influential clerical leaders who were eager to push beyond this "arrested" reformation to a more thoroughgoing reform of the church. The focal point of their immediate concern was the worship of the church, which they believed lacked theological integrity. Thus English Puritanism had its beginning as a liturgical movement. When the proposed reforms of worship were blocked by the queen, the movement split into various parties. Some people were content to tarry for the queen or her successor to act; others sought to remodel the church along presbyterian lines so that it might act independently of the sovereign; and still others—a small group of "separatists"—were determined to carry out the desired reforms "without tarrying for any" and proceeded to gather their adherents into separate congregations. A fourth and by far the most influential group was composed of preachers who busied themselves with their parish responsibilities and quietly instituted many of the desired reforms without fanfare in their own parishes.

This last course of action was made possible by a combination of factors—the reluctance of the government to take the necessary steps to enforce conformity, the inability of the bishops to exercise any real disciplinary powers, the fact that tenure in a parish was regarded as a property right which could be defended in the common law courts, and the success with which ministers were able to marshal support from among the people of their parishes. When the Stuarts, using the bishops as their agents, began to enforce an increasingly rigorous policy of conformity through the extralegal and nonecclesiastical Court of High Commission, a growing number of Puritan preachers who had been left undisturbed when they instituted liturgical reforms within their parishes were compelled for the first time to give serious attention to questions of church government. They responded by seeking to formalize in the constitution of the church the independence which they had enjoyed under Elizabeth. As a check to what they regarded as an arbitrary and even tyrannical exercise of power by a central authority, they emphasized the powers which were reserved to the individual congregation.

A Congregational Meetinghouse

The separation and reservation of powers which was to be so prominent a feature of the Constitution of the United States was characteristic of Congregationalism from the beginning, and it was a principle that was adopted for similar reasons. To guard against having ungodly ministers thrust upon unwilling congregations, it was insisted that the essence of the outward calling of a minister resides in the consent of the congregation. The second major restriction was to limit the power of excommunication to the local congregation, for it was by this means that congregations had been coerced into what they regarded as unwarranted practices. In the same way that a man charged with a civil offense could claim the right to a trial by a jury of his peers in his own community, so a man threatened by the more terrible penalty of having his soul delivered to Satan ought to have the right to be tried by those who knew him best in his own congregation.

While the negative concern for the limitation of power was a conspicuous feature of early Congregational development, an

---

STUART KINGS: Elizabeth was the last of the Tudors, and when she died the succession passed to the Stuarts. James I of Scotland became James VI of England in 1603. He was succeeded by his son, Charles I, in 1625, by whom rigorous measures to enforce religious conformity were adopted. It was during his reign that "the great migration" to Massachusetts Bay occurred. Charles I was executed in 1649, after Parliament had seized control of the nation in 1640. Charles II regained the throne for the Stuarts in 1660 and was succeeded by James II, who was deposed by the Revolution of 1688. He was replaced by William of Orange, under whom the Act of Toleration of 1689 was adopted.

CHARLES HERLE: An Anglican clergyman with presbyterian convictions. He was appointed to the Westminster Assembly in 1643 and became one of the prominent leaders of the Assembly.

GEORGE WHITEFIELD: A member of the "Holy Club" at Oxford, having been converted in 1735 through the instrumentality of Charles Wesley. He was the outstanding preacher of the Evangelical Revival and was equally famous in England and America.

equally important concern was the conviction that each believer should be given the opportunity for full and responsible participation in the life of the church. This posed the problem which had haunted Protestants from the beginning. Who among the general population could reasonably be regarded as believers and thus competent to exercise the responsibilities of the priesthood of believers in the life of the church? In early New England, as in Geneva, the force of this issue was evaded by sifting the general population so that it roughly corresponded to requirements for membership in the church. In England, however, this alternative was not a live option.

The solution of the Congregationalists to this problem was the adoption of the church covenant, after the analogy of the covenant of grace, as the basis of church life. Among the more moderate Congregationalists, the privileges of church membership were to be open to all who would covenant to "walk in the ways of Christ" with their fellow Christians; the more zealous, however, insisted that the covenant be restricted to

---

He died in Massachusetts in 1770, during his seventh visit to the American colonies.

SAMUEL DAVIES: One of the more prominent leaders of the Great Awakening in America. He was sent to Virginia as an evangelist by the presbytery of New Castle in 1747, and twelve years later he became the fourth president of the College of New Jersey, now Princeton University.

ALEXANDER CAMPBELL: The most noted and influential leader of the "Christian" movement. His father arrived in America from Ireland in 1809 and almost immediately founded the "Christian Association" of Washington, Pennsylvania. Its purpose was to unite Christians of all denominations by the restoration of the usages of the primitive church. Alexander arrived a year later and became the vigorous leader of the movement, centering his activity in western Virginia and Pennsylvania, and in eastern Ohio. Although a Presbyterian, he and his followers were for a time affiliated with the Baptists.

"such as can give some account of the work of grace wrought in them, though but in the least degree." If the members of the churches are, as Luther had suggested, to share in the determination of their own officers, the calling of their own pastors, and the judging of true preaching, it is difficult to see how the necessity for some such simple profession of their own Christian faith can be avoided.

The Congregationalists insisted that they differed from the Presbyterians only at a point at which all moderate men ought to be able to agree, and Charles Herle, a moderate Presbyterian, acknowledged that " 'tis but the better or worse way for the exercise of the same form of discipline that is in question." In similar fashion, the Baptists differed from the Congregationalists only at the point of baptism. If faith in Christ is the foundation of the Church, they were to ask, on what basis is baptism administered when the person being baptized is incapable of faith? Later they were to bring into question, not only the person, but the mode of baptism. If baptism is a sign of death and resurrection, can anything but immersion be regarded as an adequate representation of that event? Furthermore, more earnestly than some others, the Baptists took seriously the need to insure the freedom of a church to be Christ's church by rejecting completely any dependence upon the state.

2. *Methodists*

Methodism was the product of the Evangelical Revival of the eighteenth century, which in turn was the product of a renewal of the Puritan emphasis upon the necessity for personal religious experience and was motivated by a consuming passion for the redemption of mankind. Both in England and in America the parish system had broken down owing to vast movements of population, and masses of people were left completely unchurched. The revival was in essence a great home missionary campaign designed to reach these unchurched masses. The greatest preacher of the revival, in both England and America, was George Whitefield, but it was John Wesley who gave shape and structure to the Methodist phase of the awakening. Whereas

George Whitefield

Whitefield conceived his vocation as primarily to help men break through to a new birth, Wesley was equally concerned that the newborn life should be preserved and perfected.

If Wesley had chosen to relate himself to the dissenting or free churches—Presbyterian, Congregational, and Baptist—it is possible that no new denomination would have arisen. But Wesley was an Anglican and he had no intention of breaking with the Anglican Church. The Church of England, however, made no provision for the close supervision, discipline, and intimate fellowship which Wesley believed to be indispensable if the fruits of the revival were to be conserved. Thus he felt compelled to fashion societies of his own in which the new Christians could be brought together for "mutual edification" and "brotherly correction." In order that the closest watch could be kept over the new converts, these societies were further divided into classes of twelve members each with a class leader whose duty it was to supervise the personal conduct of each member according to a carefully prescribed set of rules. Tickets were issued which needed to be renewed quarterly if one were to remain in good standing. Thus a parallel organization to the established church was set up on a national scale with

John Wesley

a complete hierarchy of officers and preachers. From any administrative point of view, this was an impossible situation, and it was only a question of time until a formal separation would take place. This occurred in the United States at the Christmas Conference of 1784, while in England it did not take place until 1795.

3. *The Disciples or "Christians"*

The Disciples of Christ or the "Christian" churches were also a product of evangelicalism. A peculiar feature of evangelicalism was that it tended both to stress and to discount the importance of the external forms of church life. It emphasized the necessity of a church's being a tightly disciplined community, but it considered the particular forms adopted to serve this end to be matters largely of human preference. The fundamental ground of the Christian life was the relating of the individual soul to Christ through a personal religious experience, and in the light of this transcendent event all else was purely secondary. Thus, without exception, all the leaders of the revival stressed the common name of Christian which united them rather than the denominational labels which divided them. Said Samuel Davies:

A Christian! A Christian! Let that be your highest distinction; let that be the name which you labor to deserve. God forbid that my ministry should be the occasion of diverting your attention to anything else. . . . It has been the great object of my zeal to inculcate upon you the grand essentials of our holy religion and to make you sincere practical Christians. Alas, my dear people, unless I succeed in this, I labor to very little purpose, though I should presbyterianize the whole colony.

While the majority of evangelical leaders were not unduly disturbed by denominational divisions so long as no claims were made which tended to unchurch fellow Christians, ultimately scattered groups appeared which sought to bring an end to the divisions by restoring the usage and practice of the early church. James O'Kelley in Virginia, Abner Jones in Vermont, Thomas and Alexander Campbell in Pennsylvania, and Barton W. Stone in Kentucky all suggested that unity could be achieved if Christians would drop their party names and use only Bible names, and if they would agree to drop from their practice and worship all elements which do not have obvious Scriptural warrant. "Where the Bible speaks, we speak; where the Bible is silent, we are silent," was the essence of their program. Unfortunately, not all Christians were ready to agree to the restoration of the primitive practice alone and others differed in their interpretation as to what the primitive practice was. So, in the end, this earnest effort to secure unity resulted in the addition of one more body to the cluster of Christian denominations.

QUESTIONS TO THINK ABOUT:

1. To what extent do you believe that centralized control in the church represents a threat which must be checked by the reservation of powers to the local congregation? Is the situation different when more than one church is permitted by law to exist? Does the existence of several different denominations provide a more effective check to the exercise of arbitrary power by any one body?

2. Initially the Congregationalists and Baptists reserved only two

powers to the local congregation—ordination and excommunication. How do you account for the subsequent denial of all power to synods and associations, and a consequent emphasis upon the "autonomy" of the local church?

3. It has been suggested that local congregations are in a perilous situation when they are more fearful of the influence of a synod or a bishop than they are of "the village big-wig," for they then have no support from outside to bolster them against the pressures of non-Christian forces in their own community. In such a situation, it is contended, a White Citizens' Council or an American Legion post is able to dominate the church. How valid do you regard this contention?

4. How important do you regard Wesley's emphasis upon the necessity for adequate provision being made in the life of the church for close supervision, discipline, and intimate fellowship?

5. What do you think of the contention so conspicuous in evangelicalism that the external forms of church order are matters of relative indifference? The implication would seem to be that the whole of the Christian life is spelled out in terms of an individual's relationship to God without reference to any relationship to one's fellow Christians.

SUGGESTIONS FOR FURTHER READING:

Brief accounts of the post-Reformation churches may be found in John Dillenberger and Claude Welch, *Protestant Christianity* (Charles Scribner's Sons, 1954), pp. 99-140, and in Frederick A. Norwood, *The Development of Modern Christianity* (Abingdon Press, 1956), pp. 99-141. Thomas Hooker's summary of Congregational principles and the *Cambridge Platform* are reprinted in Williston Walker, *The Creeds and Platforms of Congregationalism* (Charles Scribner's Sons, 1893). John Wesley's *A Plain Account of the People Called Methodists* and *The Character of a Methodist* are reprinted in H. E. Fosdick, *Great Voices of the Reformation* (Random House, 1952).

IX. The Church Secures Its Freedom

The great struggle for religious freedom was fought and won in England during the Puritan Revolution from 1640 to 1660, and the victory was signalized by the adoption of the Act of Toleration in 1689. This triumph, however, was partial and incomplete, and it was in the United States that full religious freedom was first secured. Nontheological factors played a large part in fashioning the final victory, but the following pages make it clear that religious considerations were equally important.

PHILIP SCHAFF ONCE remarked that "the United States furnishes the first example in history of a government deliberately depriving itself of all legislative control over religion." He then went on to say that, in 1787, when the Constitutional Convention was held, "Congress was shut up to this course by the previous history of the American colonies and the actual condition of things at the time of the formation of the national government."

The "actual condition of things" which left no alternative to the adoption of a national policy of religious freedom was spelled out as early as 1687 by the governor of the royal colony of New York in a report to the government at home concerning the religious situation in the colony.

New York has first a chaplain, belonging to the fort, of the Church of England; secondly, a Dutch Calvinist; thirdly, a French Calvinist; fourthly, a Dutch Lutheran. Here be not many of the Church of England; few Roman Catholics; abundance of Quaker preachers, men, and women especially—Singing Quakers, Ranting Quakers; Sabbatarians; Anti-Sabbatarians; some Anabaptists; some

Jews; in short, of all sorts of opinion there are some, and the most part none at all.

"Of all sorts of opinion there are some." This was the fact that left Congress no alternative to the policy it adopted. No religious body had the clear majority which would have made a bid for preferential treatment either plausible or possible. The various religious groups had been learning to live together, and they had discovered that the only basis on which they could live together in peace was that of equal freedom for all.

A policy of religious freedom was necessary because there was such a wide diversity of religious groups. But this merely describes the facts and does not explain the event. The real question is, Why was religious diversity allowed to develop in the first place?

1. *Enriching a Trading Nation*

One thing that encouraged the development of religious diversity was the fact that the colonies, for the most part, were commercial ventures. To be profitable they had to have settlers, and a readily available source of settlers was to be found among the religiously oppressed of Europe. They desired a new home

William Penn

and were willing to run the risks of life in a new land. It was partially for this reason, we may suppose, that William Penn not only offered a sanctuary to his fellow Quakers but also sent his agents up and down the Rhineland extolling the benefits to be gained by migration to Pennsylvania.

The economic advantage to be gained from a policy of toleration was made explicit in instructions sent to Peter Stuyvesant, governor of New Amsterdam. He was reminded that the prosperity of old Amsterdam was due in no small measure to the moderation of the magistrates in dealing with religious dissent, with the consequence that "people have flocked from every land to this asylum," and he was informed that a similar policy should be pursued in New Amsterdam. "It is our opinion that some connivance would be useful, and that the consciences of men, at least, ought to remain free and unshackled." Similar instructions were sent by the Lords of Trade in London to the Council of Virginia: "A free exercise of religion . . . is essential to enriching and improving a trading nation; it should be ever held sacred in His Majesty's colonies." Edward Seymour, Lord of the Treasury, put it more bluntly. He had received an appeal for the establishment of a college in Virginia, such as Massachusetts had in Harvard, for the training of ministers. He was reminded that Virginians, as well as New Englanders, had souls to be saved. "Souls," replied Seymour, "damn your souls; make tobacco."

2. *Dissent is Difficult to Suppress in an Empty Land*

Because there was space for everyone, John Cotton saw no basis for a charge of intolerance when Roger Williams was banished from the Bay Colony.

The jurisdiction (whence a man is banished) is but small, and the country round about it large and fruitful, where a man may make his choice of variety of more pleasant and profitable seats than he leaveth behind him. In which respect, banishment in this country is not counted so much a confinement as an enlargement.

When more overt forms of coercion than banishment were at-

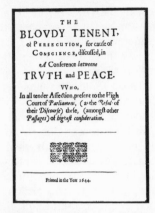

THE
BLOVDY TENENT,
of PERSECUTION, for caufe of
CONSCIENCE, difcuffed, in
A Conference *betweene*
TRVTH and PEACE.
VVHO,
In all tender Affection, prefent to the High
Court of *Parliament*, (as the *Refult* of
their *Difcourfe*) thefe, (amongft other
Paffages) of higheft confideration.

Printed in the Year 1644.

The title page of Roger Williams' famous tract of 1644.
The Bloudy Tenent of Persecution.

tempted, the open spaces of an empty land also served to make
them ineffective. Dissenters did not need to go underground;
they could just move. And they did—across the river, through
the woods, over the mountains. From the sanctuary provided
by open space and untilled acres, the contagion of dissent

ACT OF TOLERATION OF 1689:   In Great Britain the Glorious
Revolution of 1688 brought William and Mary to the throne and
resulted in the adoption of an act which extended a limited toleration to trinitarian Protestants. The enforcement of the Toleration
Act in some of the American colonies had the curious effect of
restricting rather than extending the area of toleration.

PHILIP SCHAFF: The most distinguished American church historian, who taught at Mercersburg Theological Seminary (1844-
1865) and at Union Theological Seminary in New York City
(1870-1893).

WILLIAM PENN: Quaker leader and founder of Pennsylvania,
which he regarded as a "holy experiment" in that he hoped it
might become a haven for the oppressed peoples of Europe. He
arrived with his first settlers in 1682 and died in 1718.

filtered back to the older settlements, making doubly difficult the efforts to compel conformity.

Even more important than the existence of disaffected communities as places of refuge and sources of continuing infection was the spirit and temper generated by vast stretches of empty land. A person who could always escape from the company of his fellows, if and when he wished, was not one who was apt to be unduly submissive. He thought of himself as a free man, with a mind of his own, independent of outward restraint.

3. *Theological Foundations of Freedom*

Considerations of economics and geography played their part in allowing religious diversity to develop, thus making necessary the adoption of a national policy of religious freedom. But this is only half the story. Certainly in the French and Spanish colonies the pressures of profit and space were successfully restrained. They were strongly Roman Catholic. The different policy pursued in the English colonies is explained in part by religious indifference in government circles and in part by the fact that Englishmen were developing an aversion to religious coercion. The striking feature of this growing sentiment

---

JOHN COTTON: One of the most influential of the early Congregational ministers of New England. He arrived in Boston in 1633 and died in 1652.

ROGER WILLIAMS: Regarded as a "firebrand in Israel" because he challenged the Massachusetts authorities at several points, Williams was banished from the colony and founded the earliest Rhode Island settlement at Providence in 1636, where he became known as the great apostle of religious liberty.

FRANCIS MAKEMIE: The father of American Presbyterianism, having been sent to the colonies as a missionary in 1683. He is remembered for his stirring defense of religious liberty when he was arrested by the governor of New York in 1707 for preaching without a license.

for toleration was that so much of it rested upon a sound theological basis.

This is a difficult point for many people to understand. Nathaniel Ward of Ipswich found it puzzling, for he believed that a person who "is willing to tolerate any religion . . . either doubts his own or is not sincere in it." Furthermore, it seemed clear to him that anyone who "is willing to tolerate any unsound opinion that his own may also be tolerated, though never so sound, will for a need hang God's Bible at the Devil's girdle."

There is much to be said for Ward's point of view. Tolerance is often the product of indifference. People are tolerant in those areas in which they have no strong convictions. And religious indifference did contribute to the achievement of religious freedom in America. The puzzling question, however, is why many who were not religiously indifferent should have joined so wholeheartedly in the struggle for religious freedom. The answer is to be found in three fundamental theological convictions.

Federal Hall, New York City, where the Bill of Rights
was adopted.

First of all, *the church must be free*—free to determine its own life, to define the basis of its membership, to speak God's word of judgment, to sound God's summons to repentance, to endeavor to shape the life of the total community according to its understanding of God's will. In other words, the church must be free to strive, however imperfectly, to be Christ's church. Christ is the head of the church, and Christ is the sole authority to which the church must yield obedience. To subject the church to the control and direction of the state, said one of the New England divines, would be "to pull God and Christ and Spirit out of heaven, and subject them unto natural, sinful, inconstant men, and so consequently to Satan himself, by whom all peoples naturally are guided."

Secondly, if a church must be free to strive to be Christ's church, *it must be prepared to grant the same freedom to other churches*. This is no mere doctrine of expedience, for it rests upon the assumption that there may be something to be learned from others.

In the Protestant understanding of the divine economy, no mortal man and no human institution can be regarded as infallible. As the Form of Government adopted by the Presbyterian Church was to put it, even ecclesiastical assemblies are composed of "fallible men," and therefore it must be acknowledged that "all synods and councils may err, through the frailty inseparable from humanity." Not even the self-disclosure of God in Scripture, John Calvin had insisted, could be regarded as self-explanatory. The understanding of divine truth is dependent upon the gift of the Holy Spirit, and no one can be absolutely certain of possessing the Spirit. Thus an element of humility and tentativeness must always be present in Protestant formulations of faith. "We doubt not what we practice," said Thomas Hooker of Connecticut, "but it's beyond all doubt, that all men are liars, and we are in the number of those poor feeble men, either we do or may err, though we do not know it, what we have learned we do profess, and yet profess still to live, that we may learn."

From the 1640's on, there had been an increasing insistence

that the only way God's will could be disclosed and confirmed was through unfettered discussion. One Puritan leader asked: "How can truth appear but by argumentation?" Another one wrote: "We have a proverb that they that will find must as well seek where a thing is not, as where it is. . . . And this liberty of free disquisition is as great a means to keep the truth as to find it. The running water keeps pure and clear, when the standing pool corrupts."

God's will is made known through discussion, because his Spirit is no respecter of persons. Light might break forth from "the meanest of the brethren." Truth might be perceived by any man. Every man, therefore, must be free to be convinced and in turn to convince.

Lastly, it was insisted, *the church must be granted no coercive power*. This was a corollary of the recognition that all men are in bondage to sin and subject to the temptation to exalt themselves in rebellion against God. Said John Cotton:

Let all the world learn to give mortal man no greater power than they are content they shall use, for use it they will. . . . It is necessary that all power that is on earth be limited, church power or other. . . . It is counted a matter of danger to the state to limit prerogatives, but it is a further danger not to have them limited.

As Cotton implied, the limitation of power is necessary in every area of life, and the experience of most early Americans had taught them that political absolutism and ecclesiastical absolutism were equally to be feared. Thus, while it was necessary to limit the power of the state, it was also necessary to limit the power of the church. Therefore, Cotton insisted that to give any power of coercion to the church would be to make "the church a monster." Governments, he continued, create a "monstrous deformity" when they surrender any of their authority to the church, so that if the church condemns anyone, they must do so too. And it was for this reason that the Presbyterians stated very explicitly that "ecclesiastical discipline" must not be "attended with any civil effects" and "can derive no force whatever but from its own justice, the approbation of an impartial public, and the countenance and blessing of the great Head of the Church Universal." The only power at the disposal of the church is the influence it may exert by persuasion.

Even the best of men do not always see the full implications of their basic convictions nor do they always live up to them. Freedom was not won without a struggle. When freedom was denied, there were many to respond as did Francis Makemie

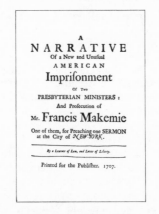

A

NARRATIVE
Of a New and Unuſual
AMERICAN
Impriſonment
Of Two
PRESBYTERIAN MINISTERS :
And Proſecution of
Mr. Francis Makemie
One of them, for Preaching one SERMON
at the City of *NEW YORK*.

By a Learner of Law, and Lover of Liberty.

Printed for the Publiſher. 1707.

The title page of Francis Makemie's account of his
arrest and imprisonment.

when he declared: "To give bond not to preach . . . if invited by the people, we neither can nor dare do it." A right which is claimed for oneself, however, is not always extended to others. It was because men are fallible and inconstant, and because "God alone is Lord of the conscience," that the Presbyterians, for example, insisted that they did "not even wish to see any religious constitution aided by the civil power, further than may be necessary for protection and security." The sole responsibility of the state was to make sure that no one, "either upon pretense of religion or infidelity," be permitted "to offer any indignity, violence, abuse, or injury to any other person whatsoever," and to take proper precautions to insure that "all religious and ecclesiastical assemblies be held without molestation or disturbance."

QUESTIONS TO THINK ABOUT:

1. What were the most basic reasons for the development of religious freedom in America?

2. Is the problem of preserving our freedom apt to become more acute now that the United States is no longer largely an empty land?

3. What is the relation of religious freedom to freedom of speech and freedom of the press?

4. James Madison, in the *Federalist Papers,* asserted that the surest guarantee of religious freedom "consists in a multiplicity of sects." Do you agree? Is this an adequate guarantee?

5. Why is it important for a church to assert its own freedom? Why is it important for a church to defend the freedom of other churches or religious bodies?

SUGGESTIONS FOR FURTHER READING:

A more extended discussion of this theme is to be found in W. S. Hudson, *The Great Tradition of the American Churches* (Harper & Brothers, 1953). The conditioning influence of the American environment is discussed perceptively by Sidney E. Mead, "The American People: Their Space, Time, and Religion," *Journal of Religion,* October, 1954. A selection from Roger Williams' *Bloudy Tenent of Persecution* is reprinted in H. E. Fosdick, *Great Voices of the Reformation* (Random House, 1952).

x. The Church and the Churches

Religious "sects" often claim the authority of the Bible or of Christian tradition exclusively for themselves. By definition a sect is exclusive—separate. Thus the Reformers spoke of "the great sect of Rome." Protestants have not been immune to sectarian tendencies, but these tendencies do run counter to what has become the dominant current in Protestantism. This final chapter, by tracing the development of this current in Protestantism, shows the persistent concern of the churches to make manifest the unity they have in Christ.

NO CHRISTIAN HAS ever been happy about the divisions which exist among the churches, and every age has witnessed earnest and devoted efforts to bring them to an end. On the other hand, even in the midst of their divisions, Christians have repeatedly affirmed that the body of Christ, which is the Church, has not and cannot be divided. Thus when they sing, "We are not divided, all one body we," and "Elect from every nation, yet one o'er all the earth," Christians are not indulging in pious hypocrisy but are expressing what to them is an actual reality. For, from the perspective of the Protestant understanding of the nature of the Church, neither the continuity nor the unity of the Church depends ultimately upon outward ecclesiastical forms. The true succession is a succession of believers, and the real unity is the unity that is found in Christ wherever faith has been awakened.

1. *The Denominational Theory of the Church*

In his preface to *The Institutes of the Christian Religion,* John Calvin confessed that there are many who "are not satisfied unless the Church can always be pointed out with the finger." But this, he continued, is something that cannot be done in any final sense. The whole question as to the dimensions, the boundaries, the limits of the Church of Christ must be left to God, "since he alone 'knoweth them that are his.' " In similar fashion, Luther's fundamental criticism of Roman Catholicism was that it had sought to imprison Christ within man-made historical forms. While it is inevitable and necessary that the Church shall find institutional expression "in a place and in the things and activities of the world," said Luther, "yet it is not properly understood in terms of all this. . . . For as in this life the Church is not without eating and drinking and yet the Kingdom of God, according to Paul, does not consist of eating and drinking, so the Church is not without place and body and yet the place and body do not make the Church and do not constitute it." The external ecclesiastical arrangements ought to be of such an order that they do not block the free course of the Word of God in the world, but Luther never doubted that men could be found by Christ even under conditions in which he was misinterpreted and the gospel perverted and defiled.

Luther and Calvin acted upon this insight only to a limited degree. It was useful in their criticism of Romanist pretensions, but the broad-minded spirit it implied did not lead them to suppose that men who honestly differed in their apprehension of Christ should be tolerated and allowed to pursue unmolested their own understanding of the implications of the gospel. It was left for a later generation to acknowledge the "deceitfulness" which forever lurks within the human heart and to point out that so long as men live "in this muddy world," it will be impossible for them to dogmatize concerning their apprehension of the ways in which Christ would have them walk. The peculiar circumstances of time and place color and distort the apprehensions even of the best of men. The "Dissenting Brethren" of the Westminster Assembly, having gone into exile, believed that this circumstance had served to free them from bias and thus had allowed them to search out the proper pattern of church government with impartiality, being guided only by the "light and touch" of God's Spirit.

> We had, of all men, the greatest reason to be true to our own consciences . . . , seeing that it was for our conscience that we were deprived at once of whatever was dear to us. We had no new commonwealths to rear to frame the church unto. . . . We had no state-ends or political interests to comply with; no kingdoms in our eye to subdue to our mold . . . ; no preferments or worldly respects to shape our opinion for. We had nothing else to do but simply and singly to consider how to worship God acceptably and so most according to his Word.

In spite of the favorable situation for impartial inquiry in which they found themselves, they remembered "our own frailty in the former way of our conformity" and therefore they were determined to keep a "reserve to alter or retract (though not lightly) whatever should be discovered to be taken up out of a misunderstanding of the rule."

It was by such men who had become "privy to their own infirmities" and who were "far from dreaming of perfection in this life" that the denominational theory of the church was developed. It was an answer to the dilemma created by the fact that a Christian must profess and practice according to the light that had been given him, and yet must not be so presumptuous as to deny the possibility that other men more "eminently gifted" might have "dug deeper" and found further light. An easy tolerance, born of indifference and expressing itself in ecclesiastical laxity, would not do, for Christians must pursue and practice the implications of their faith as they understand it. But while professing and practicing their own understanding of the gospel, they must not deny the same right to others from whom perchance they have much to learn.

The Reformers, to be sure, did deal with the problem to a limited degree. They were willing to recognize as true churches all churches that possessed an essentially evangelical faith, whether they were Lutheran churches in Germany and Scandinavia; Reformed churches in Switzerland, Holland, and Scotland; or an Anglican church in England. All these churches in their various geographical areas were seen as different *manifestations* of the one holy catholic Church of Christ which embraced them all. The point at which the Reformers hesitated was when religious diversity existed within a particular geographical area rather than between different geographical areas. They found it difficult to acknowledge that churches of differing church order located on opposite corners in the same city could be regarded as sharing in the life of the whole Church. Yet this was implicit in the whole structure of Reformation thinking concerning the nature of the Church.

The hesitancy of the Reformers to pursue the full implications of their thinking was overcome in that current of Puritanism which stressed inward religious experience as fundamental to the Christian life, and in the related movements of Pietism and Evangelicalism. Typical of the sentiment which came rapidly to the fore are John Wesley's oft-quoted words: "I . . . refuse to be distinguished from other men by any but the common principles of Christianity. . . . I renounce and detest all other marks of distinction. But from real Christians, of whatever

---

ALBERT BARNES: Minister of the historic First Presbyterian Church of Philadelphia for forty years (1830-1870) and the foremost leader of the New School or evangelical party among the Presbyterians. It is reported that more than one million copies of his commentaries were printed and sold.

NATIONAL COUNCIL OF CHURCHES: After 1900 a cluster of official interdenominational agencies were formed to coordinate the work of the various Protestant denominations in North America. Among these bodies were the Home Missions Council, the International Council of Religious Education, the United Stewardship Council, the Council of Church Women, and the Federal Council of Churches. Taken together these various agencies, including the Foreign Missions Conference which had been formed just prior to 1900, provided the means for co-ordinating every aspect of the work of the member churches. There was some overlapping and duplication of effort, however, and in 1950 they were replaced by two general agencies—the National Council of Churches in the United States and the Canadian Council of Churches.

denomination, I earnestly desire not to be distinguished at all. . . . Dost thou love and fear God? It is enough! I give thee the right hand of fellowship." A century later Albert Barnes, minister of the First Presbyterian Church of Philadelphia, summed up the common conviction when he declared: "The spirit of this age . . . is opposed to all bigotry and uncharitableness; to all attempts to 'unchurch' others; to teaching that they worship in conventicles, that they are dissenters, or that they are left to the uncovenanted mercies of God. . . . The Church of Christ is not under the Episcopal form, or the Baptist, the Methodist, the Presbyterian, or the Congregational form exclusively; all are, to all intents and purposes, to be recognized as parts of the one holy catholic Church."

What, then, is denominationalism? It is the opposite of sectarianism. The basic contention of the denominational theory of the church is that the true Church is not to be identified exclusively with any single ecclesiastical structure. No denomination claims to represent the whole Church of Christ.

WORLD COUNCIL OF CHURCHES: Several currents of interest combined to produce the World Council of Churches. The first stemmed directly from the mission fields, where the divisions among Christians imported from the West seriously impaired the task of evangelism and unnecessarily weakened the small Christian communities which were struggling to maintain themselves in non-Christian societies. This interest culminated in the International Missionary Conference at Edinburgh in 1910, which gave birth to two differing approaches to unity—one seeking to come to terms with issues of Faith and Order, and the other seeking to secure practical co-operation in Life and Work. Another strand of interest was provided by the World Student Christian Federation. Leaders in all these areas became accustomed to working together, and the World Council of Churches which was formed at Amsterdam in 1948 was the product of their combined efforts. At the Evanston meeting of the World Council in 1954, representatives were present from 163 churches of 48 different countries.

No denomination claims that all other churches are false churches. Each denomination can be and should be regarded as constituting no more than a different "mode" of expressing in piety, thought, and organization that larger life of the Church in which they all share. The word "denomination" to describe a religious communion was adopted by the leaders of the Evangelical Revival simply because it was a neutral or ecumenical term carrying with it no implication of a negative value judgment and because it implied that the group referred to is but one member, called or denominated by a particular name, of a larger group—the Church—to which all denominations belong.

2. Paths to Unity

The denominational theory of the church presupposed that all denominations would co-operate in freedom and mutual respect in discharging their tasks as churches of Christ. This the denominations proceeded to do.

In the United States the nineteenth century was an age of co-operative activities among the churches. Following the pattern established in the preceding century by Whitefield, practically all of the great revivals of the nineteenth century were carried on with little attention to denominational affiliation. In addition to joint sponsorship of revival campaigns, voluntary societies were created to meet almost every type of need—the American Board of Commissioners for Foreign Missions, the American Home Mission Society, the American Bible Society, the American Tract Society, the American Temperance Society, the American Peace Society, the American Education Society, the American Anti-Slavery Society. Later in the century there were the numerous city mission societies, the Y.M.C.A. and the Y.W.C.A., the Student Volunteer Movement, the International Society of Christian Endeavor, and the astonishing mass Sunday School Movement which penetrated to the very heart of the life of the individual denominations and bound the members of different churches together with the bond of "next Sunday's lesson" and joint teacher-training institutes.

By the twentieth century practically all these agencies had been supplemented by denominational societies and boards, which in turn were linked by joint councils and conferences of one type or another, and ultimately these separate councils were to be brought together to form the National Council of Churches. Thus the National Council of Churches is the heir of the co-operative activities of the nineteenth century and an expression of the continued determination of the denominations to work together in freedom and mutual respect. Similar in character and intention is the World Council of Churches, and also the various local and state councils.

While we cannot expect, so long as we live in this "muddy world," to realize the full unity we have in Christ in a single comprehensive ecclesiastical structure which shall embrace all Christians, this does not mean that Christians can ever be content merely to carry on co-operative activities. The perpetuation of divisions that have no basis in honestly held convictions which relate to an understanding of the mind of Christ cannot be justified. Nor does the fact that there will always be differing apprehensions of the mind of Christ free us from the obligation to seek to reconcile—through study, discussion, and prayer—the differences of honestly held convictions which do exist. It is significant that the World Council of Churches should regard the provision of opportunities for study and discussion as one of its major contributions to the cause of Christian unity, and the increasing degree to which Christians of various denominations are finding themselves in substantial agreement is one of the most heartening features of our time.

3. *What of the Future?*

In the years immediately ahead, present trends would indicate that the denominations will manifest a greater degree of outward unity through co-operative activities, in new provisions for intercommunion and the mutual recognition of ministries, and in actual organic union of existing denominations. At a time when the nations of the world have been drawn into "blocs" of varying degrees of hostility toward one another,

Christians throughout the world have been drawn closer together. This is the great fact of the Ecumenical Movement.

The strong tide of increased fellowship and unity among Christians of different nations has been paralleled by a similar movement among Christians within the various countries. In the United States, apart from the formation of the National Council of Churches, this has been the record:

In 1911 the Northern Baptists and the Free Baptists united, in 1917 three Lutheran bodies came together to form the United Lutheran Church; in the same year two Norwegian Lutheran bodies united; in 1920 the Welsh Calvinistic Methodists united with the northern Presbyterians; in 1922 two groups came together to form the Evangelical Church; in 1924 the Hungarian Reformed Church united with the Reformed Church in the United States; in 1930 three Lutheran bodies came together to form the American Lutheran Church; in 1931 the Congregational and Christian Churches united; in 1934 the Evangelical and Reformed Church was formed as a result of the union of the Evangelical Synod and the Reformed Church in the United States; in 1939 three Methodist bodies were reunited; in 1946 the Evangelical Church and the United Brethren in Christ came together to form the Evangelical United Brethren Church; in 1957 the General Council of the Congregational Christian Churches and the General Synod of the Evangelical and Reformed Church voted to unite; and in the same year the United Presbyterian Church and the Presbyterian Church U.S.A. voted to proceed with plans for union.

What has been true in the United States has also been true in England, Scotland, France, and among many of the "younger churches" of the mission fields. Even more dramatic unions have occurred in Canada, where Congregationalists, Methodists, and Presbyterians were brought together to form the United Church of Canada; and in India, where Anglicans were numbered among those uniting to form the Church of South India.

Outward unity, however, must never be an end in itself; it has its justification only when it enables Christians more effectively to bear witness to Christ and to the unity they find in him. Christ is the Lord of the Church and he must never be allowed to be imprisoned in the structures we fashion in his name. The possible necessity of a new reformation, involving a sharp break with and dissent from an existing Christian community, must never be ruled out. Our unity is in Christ, and our pre-eminent task is to "study Christ," to be open to the leading of his Spirit, and to walk in the light which is made known to us.

QUESTIONS TO THINK ABOUT:

1. Is the real unity of the Church to be found in organization? If not, where is the unity of the Church to be found?

2. The Reformers frequently referred to "the great sect of Rome." Why did they regard Rome as sectarian? How would you distinguish between sectarianism and denominationalism?

3. How do the denominations serve to correct the pretensions of any single denomination?

4. How would you explain Luther's contention that true Christians are to be found even in churches that misinterpret and pervert the gospel?

5. What is meant when it is said that the first word of a church must be a word against itself? Of what must a church repent?

6. Why should missionaries feel most keenly the need for Christian unity?

SUGGESTIONS FOR FURTHER READING:

A brief account of the Ecumenical Movement is given in John Dillenberger and Claude Welch, *Protestant Christianity* (Charles Scribner's Sons, 1954), pp. 284-301. A fuller discussion is Robert S. Bilheimer, *The Quest for Christian Unity* (Association Press, 1952). The constitution of the World Council of Churches is printed in *The First Assembly of the World Council of Churches*, W. A. Visser t'Hooft, ed. (Harper & Brothers, 1949). The plan of union for the United Church of Canada is printed in G. K. A. Bell, *Documents on Christian Unity, 1920-24* (Oxford University Press, 1924), and that of South India is given in B. G. M. Sundkler, *The Church of South India* (Lutterworth Press, 1954).

Chronological Table

(The early dates are only approximate)

26–29	The Crucifixion
35	Conversion of Paul
64	Neronian Persecution
70	Destruction of Jerusalem
250	Decian Persecution
303	Outbreak of Diocletian Persecution
312	Constantine's Victory at Milvian Bridge
313	Edict of Milan
325	Council of Nicea
358	Monastic Rule drafted by Basil of Caesarea
374	Ambrose becomes bishop of Milan
392	Theodosius proscribes pagan worship
410	Fall of Rome
426	Augustine completes *City of God*
440	Leo I becomes bishop of Rome and formulates Petrine theory
526	Benedict of Nursia establishes monasticism in the West
590	Gregory the Great becomes bishop of Rome
800	Coronation of Charlemagne as Holy Roman Emperor
1054	Rome breaks with the Eastern churches
1073	Hildebrand (Gregory VII) becomes bishop of Rome
1096	First Crusade
1176	Peter Waldo begins preaching
1209	Francis of Assisi gathers his first followers
1215	Magna Carta

1232	Inquisition established
1309	The papacy at Avignon
1378	Great Schism, with two rival popes, begins
1382	John Wyclif translates the Bible
1409	Council of Pisa
1415	John Hus burned at the stake
1417	Council of Constance ends the Great Schism
1498	Savonarola executed
1506	Reuchlin's Hebrew grammar
1516	Erasmus' Greek New Testament
1517	Luther's Ninety-five Theses
1521	Luther appears before Diet of Worms
1522	Zwingli begins Reformation in Zurich
1534	England completes its break with Rome
1536	Calvin arrives in Geneva
1545	Council of Trent redefines the Roman position
1558	Accession of Queen Elizabeth
1560	John Knox leads Scottish Reformation
1603	James VI of Scotland becomes James I of England
1630	"Great migration" to Massachusetts Bay
1640	Long Parliament meets
1642	English Civil War begins
1643	Westminster Assembly meets
1649	Charles I executed
1660	Charles II restored to English throne
1689	English Act of Toleration
1726	Great Awakening in America begins with preaching of Theodore J. Frelinghuysen
1734	Revival at Northampton under Jonathan Edwards
1739	John Wesley begins field preaching
1910	Edinburgh International Missionary Conference
1948	World Council of Churches formed at Amsterdam

Index

Alexander VI, 52
Ambrose, 20 f., 23, 30
Anglican communion, 30
Apologetical Narration, 62
Apostles, 7, 11 f.
Apostolic succession, 28 f., 36
Apostolic witness, 7, 11 f.
Avignon, 43, 45 f.

Baillie, John, 20
Baptism, 21, 78
Baptists, 61, 64, 73, 77-79, 81,
    100
Barker, Ernest, 24
Barnes, Albert, 96 f.
Basel, Council of, 47
Basil of Caesarea, 40
Benedict IX, 31
Bevan, Edwyn, 17
Book of Martyrs, 53, 60
Boston, ministers of, 28
Brethren of the Common Life,
    40 f., 42

Calvin, John, 52, 68 f., 89, 93 f.
Campbell, Alexander and
    Thomas, 77, 81
Canada, United Church of, 100
Canadian Council of Churches,
    100
Canossa, 29, 35
Case, S. J., 24
Charlemagne, 28, 31

Charles I, 76
Christian unity, 93, 96-101
Church: as New Israel, 2 f., 7;
    as people of God, 1-3, 7 f., 44,
    55-57, 67, 93-98; covenant, 77
    f.; freedom of, 24 f., 30-32,
    64-68, 70, 73, 78, 83-92; in-
    stitution, 3 f.; organization of,
    8-11, 27-30, 44-46, 61-71, 73-
    81, 89-92, 94-98
Clement VII, 45
Clerical celibacy, 32
Clericalism, 22, 53-55, 63, 66
College of Cardinals, 29, 32
Conciliarists, 41, 42-47
Congregationalists, 61, 64, 73-
    78, 79, 81, 100
Constance, Council of, 46 f.
Constantine, 16-25, 30, 47
Constantinople, 20, 30
Cotton, John, 36, 85, 87, 90
Court of High Commission, 75
Cranmer, Thomas, 64, 66 f.
Cyprian, 28

Damascus, 23
Dante, 47 f.
Davies, Samuel, 77, 81
Denominationalism, 73, 93-97
Didache, 8, 10
Disciples of Christ, 61, 73, 77,
    80 f.

Dissenting Brethren, 62, 64, 94 f.
Donation of Constantine, 47 f.

Eastern churches, 30
Edinburgh Conference of 1910, 97; of 1937, 1, 3
Elizabeth I, 52, 74-76
England, Church of, 25, 52, 61, 64, 65-68, 74, 76, 79, 83
Evangelical revivals, 38-42, 73, 76-81
Evangelicalism, 73, 76, 78-81, 96, 98

Figgis, J. N., 24
Foxe, John, 53, 60
Francis of Assisi, 39 f., 40, 42 f.
Franciscans, 41, 43
Franck, Sebastian, 48
Friends of God, 40, 42

Garrison, W. E., 16
Geneva, 69, 71, 73, 77
Gerson, John, 41, 44
Gregory I, 28, 30; VI, 31 f.; VII (Hildebrand), 29, 31-35, 47; IX, 41; XI, 45

Henry III, 31; IV, 29, 33, 35
Herle, Charles, 76, 78
Hildebrand, *see* Gregory VII
Hobbes, Thomas, 34
Hooker, Richard, 65
Hooker, Thomas, 89
Hus, John, 42

Indulgences, 54 f.
Innocent III, 34 f.; VIII, 51
Inquisition, 41, 43 f.
Ireland, 30
Irenaeus, 28

James I of England (James VI of Scotland), 65, 76
Jerome, 17, 19 f., 40
Jewel, John, 65, 67
John XXII, 41, 43
John of England, 34 f.
John of Paris, 41, 43
Jones, Abner, 81
Justin Martyr, 8
Justinian, Code of, 44

Kirk, K. E., 17
Knox, John, 52, 65, 69 f.

Latimer, Hugh, 53, 59
Latourette, K. S., 27
Leo I, 28; IX, 32; X, 52, 57 f.
Lorenzo the Magnificent, 52 f.
Luther, Martin, 5, 50, 52-59, 62-65, 68, 78, 94
Lutheran churches, 25, 61, 63-66, 68, 83, 100

Madison, James, 92
Magna Carta, 35
Makemie, Francis, 87, 91
Martin V, 46 f.
Martyrs, 13, 58-60
Mary of England, 53, 64 f.
Mary of Scotland, 70
Melanchthon, 58
Melville, Andrew, 65, 69
Methodists, 61, 73, 78-80, 100
Monasticism, 40-42

National Council of Churches, 96, 99
Nazi regime, 25
Neill, Stephen, 47 f.
New Testament Canon, 8-9, 11-12

Nichols, J. H., 36, 37, 57
Ninety-five Theses, 50, 52, 57

O'Kelley, James, 81

Papacy, 27-35, 41-48, 51-55
Paul, the Apostle, 5, 10, 94
Penn, William, 85 f.
Petrine succession, 27-30, 36
Pietism, 96
Pisa, Council of, 46
Presbyterians, 61, 64 f., 68-71, 74, 77-79, 81, 90 f., 100
Priesthood of believers, 56 f., 63, 66-68, 77
Puritanism, 62, 64, 73-75, 78, 83, 90, 96

Quakers, 83, 85

Reformed churches, 67-71, 83
Religious diversity, 83-87
Religious freedom, 83, 87-92, 95
Ridley, Nicholas, 53, 59
Rome, Church of, 27-36, 41-48, 93, 94
Royal supremacy, 66-68
Russia, Church of, 25

Sacramentalism, 20-22
Schaff, Philip, 83, 86
Scotland, Church of, 52, 64 f., 69-71, 73
Sectarianism, 93
Separatists, 74

Seymour, Edward, 85
Shepherd of Hermas, 1, 3
South India, Church of, 100
Stephen, 12
Stone, Barton W., 81
Stuyvesant, Peter, 85
Sylvester I, 47; III, 31

Tetzel, Johann, 53-55
Theodosius, 21, 24
Toleration, Act of, 76, 83, 86
Toynbee, Arnold, 33 f.

United States Constitution, 76, 83 f.
Urban VI, 45

Waldo, Peter, 40, 42
Ward, Nathaniel, 87
Wesley, Charles, 76
Wesley, John, 78-80, 82, 96
Westminster Assembly, 62, 64, 94
Whitefield, George, 76-79, 98
Whitgift, John, 65, 67
William of Ockham, 41, 45
William of Orange, 52, 76
William the Conqueror, 34
Williams, Roger, 85 f., 87
World Council of Churches, 97, 99
Wyclif, John, 42

Zwingli, Huldreich, 52

118306